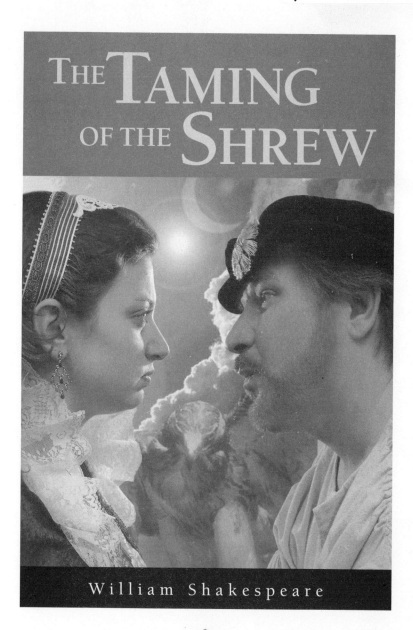

THE TAMING OF THE SHREW

William Shakespeare

Prestwick House
LITERARY TOUCHSTONE CLASSICS™

P.O. Box 658 Clayton, Delaware 19938 • www.prestwickhouse.com

SENIOR EDITOR: Paul Moliken

EDITORS: Elizabeth Osborne, Lisa M. Miller

COVER IMAGE: Wendy Smith

DESIGN & PRODUCTION: Chris Koniencki

Prestwick House
LITERARY TOUCHSTONE CLASSICS™

P.O. BOX 658 • CLAYTON, DELAWARE 19938
TEL: 1.800.932.4593
FAX: 1.888.718.9333
WEB: www.prestwickhouse.com

Prestwick House Teaching Units™, Activity Packs™, and Response Journals™ are the perfect complement for these editions. To purchase teaching resources for this book, visit www.prestwickhouse.com

ISBN 978-1-58049-592-9

CONTENTS

Strategies for Understanding Shakespeare's Language

1. When reading verse, note the appropriate phrasing and intonation.

   DO NOT PAUSE AT THE END OF A LINE unless there is a mark of punctuation. Shakespearean verse has a rhythm of its own, and once a reader gets used to it, the rhythm becomes very natural to speak in and read. Beginning readers often find it helpful to read a short pause at a comma and a long pause for a period, colon, semicolon, dash, or question mark.
   Here's an example from *The Merchant of Venice*, Act IV, Scene i:

   > The quality of mercy is not strain'd, (*short pause*)
   > It droppeth as the gentle rain from heaven
   > Upon the place beneath: (*long pause*) it is twice blest; (*long pause*)
   > It blesseth him that gives, (*short pause*) and him that takes; (*long pause*)
   > 'Tis mightiest in the mighties; (*long pause*) it becomes
   > The throned monarch better than his crown; (*long pause*)

2. Read from punctuation mark to punctuation mark for meaning.

   In addition to helping you read aloud, punctuation marks define units of thought. Try to understand each unit as you read, keeping in mind that periods, colons, semicolons, and question marks signal the end of a thought. Here's an example from *The Taming of the Shrew*, Act I, Scene i:

   > Luc. Tranio, I saw her coral lips to move,
   >   And with her breath she did perfume the air;
   >   Sacred, and sweet, was all I saw in her.
   > Tra. Nay, then, 'tis time to stir him from his trance.
   >   I pray, awake, sir: if you love the maid,
   >   Bend thoughts and wits to achieve her.

   The first unit of thought is from "Tranio" to "air":

He saw her lips move, and her breath perfumed the air.

The second thought ("Sacred, and sweet...") re-emphasizes the first.

Tranio replies that Lucentio needs to awaken from his trance and try to win "the maid." These two sentences can be considered one unit of thought.

3. In an **inverted sentence**, the verb comes before the subject. Some lines will be easier to understand if you put the subject first and reword the sentence. For example, look at the line below:

   "*Never was seen so black a day as this:*" (*Romeo and Juliet*, Act IV, Scene v)

   You can change its inverted pattern so it is more easily understood:

   "*A day as black as this was never seen:*"

4. An **ellipsis** occurs when a word or phrase is left out. In *Romeo and Juliet*, Benvolio asks Romeo's father and mother if they know the problem that is bothering their son. Romeo's father answers:

   "*I neither know **it** nor can learn of **him***" (*Romeo and Juliet*, Act I, Scene i)

   This sentence can easily be understood to mean,

   "*I neither know [the cause of] it,
   nor can [I] learn [about it from] him.*"

5. As you read longer speeches, keep track of the subject, verb, and object—who did what to whom.

   In the clauses below, note the subject, verbs, and objects:

   Ross: The king hath happily received, Macbeth,
   The news of thy success: and when he reads
   Thy personal venture in the rebel's fight... (*Macbeth*, Act I, Scene iii)

   1st clause: *The king hath happily received, Macbeth,/The news of thy success:*
   SUBJECT – The king
   VERB – has received
   OBJECT – the news [of Macbeth's success]

2nd clause: *and when he reads/thy personal venture in the rebel's fight,*
SUBJECT – he [the king]
VERB – reads
OBJECT – [about] your venture

In addition to following the subject, verb, and object of a clause, you also need to track pronoun references. In the following soliloquy, Romeo, who is madly in love with Juliet, secretly observes her as she steps out on her balcony. To help you keep track of the pronoun references, we've made margin notes. (Note that the feminine pronoun sometimes refers to Juliet, but sometimes does not.)

> But, soft! what light through yonder window breaks?
> It is the east, and Juliet is the sun!
> Arise, fair sun, and kill the envious moon,
> Who* is already sick and pale with grief,   *"Who" refers to the moon.*
> That thou her* maid* art more fair than she:*   *"thou her maid" refers*
>   *to Juliet, the sun.*
>   *"she" and "her" refer to the moon.*

In tracking the line of action in a passage, it is useful to identify the main thoughts that are being expressed and paraphrase them. Note the following passage in which Hamlet expresses his feelings about the death of his father and the remarriage of his mother:

> O God! a beast that wants discourse of reason
> Would have mourn'd longer—married with my uncle,
> My father's brother, but no more like my father
> Than I to Hercules. (*Hamlet*, Act I, Scene ii)

Paraphrasing the three main points, we find that Hamlet is saying:

- a mindless beast would have mourned the death of its mate longer than my mother did
- she married my uncle, my father's brother
- my uncle is not at all like my father

If you are having trouble understanding Shakespeare, the first rule is to read it out loud, just as an actor rehearsing would have to do. That will help you understand how one thought is connected to another.

6. Shakespeare frequently uses **metaphor** to illustrate an idea in a unique way. Pay careful attention to the two dissimilar objects or ideas being compared.

In *Macbeth*, Duncan, the king says:
> I have begun to plant thee, and will labour
> To make thee full of growing. (*Macbeth*, Act I, Scene v)

The king compares Macbeth to a tree he can plant and watch grow.

7. An **allusion** is a reference to some event, person, place, or artistic work, not directly explained or discussed by the writer; it relies on the reader's familiarity with the item referred to. Allusion is a quick way of conveying information or presenting an image. In the following lines, Romeo alludes to Diana, goddess of the hunt and of chastity, and to Cupid's arrow (love).

> ROMEO: Well, in that hit you miss: she'll not be hit
> with Cupid's arrow, she hath Dian's wit;
> and in strong proof of chastity well arm'd
> (*Romeo and Juliet*, Act I, Scene i)

8. Contracted words are words in which a letter has been left out. Some that frequently appear:

be't	on't	wi'	do't
t'	'sblood	'gainst	ta'en
i'	'tis	e'en	'bout
know'st	'twill	ne'er	o'
o'er			

9. Archaic, obsolete, and familiar words with unfamiliar definitions may also cause problems.

- **Archaic Words:** Some archaic words, like *thee*, *thou*, *thy*, and *thine*, are instantly understandable, while others, like *betwixt*, cause a momentary pause.

- **Obsolete Words:** If it were not for the notes in a Shakespeare text, obsolete words could be a problem; words like *beteem* are usually not found in student dictionaries. In these situations, however, a quick glance at the book's notes will solve the problem.

- **Familiar Words with Unfamiliar Definitions:** Another problem is those familiar words whose definitions have changed. Because readers think they know the word, they do not check the notes. For example, in this comment from *Much Ado About Nothing*, Act I, Scene i, the word *an* means "if":

BEATRICE: Scratching could not make it worse, *an* 'twere such
a face as yours were.

For this kind of word, we have included margin notes.

10. Wordplay—puns, double entendres, and malapropisms:

- A **pun** is a literary device that achieves humor or emphasis by playing on ambiguities. Two distinct meanings are suggested either by the same word or by two similar-sounding words.

- A **double entendre** is a kind of pun in which a word or phrase has a second, usually sexual, meaning.

- A **malapropism** occurs when a character mistakenly uses a word that he or she has confused with another word. In *Romeo and Juliet*, the Nurse tells Romeo that she needs to have a "confidence" with him, when she should have said "conference." Mockingly, Benvolio then says she probably will "indite" (rather than "invite") Romeo to dinner.

11. Shakespeare's Language:

Our final word on Shakespeare's language is adapted by special permission from Ralph Alan Cohen's book *Shakesfear and How to Cure It—A Guide to Teaching Shakespeare.*

What's so hard about Shakespeare's language? Many students come to Shakespeare's language assuming that the language of his period is substantially different from ours. In fact, 98% of the words in Shakespeare are current-usage English words. So why does it sometimes seem hard to read Shakespeare? There are three main reasons:

- Originally, Shakespeare wrote the words for an actor to illustrate them as he spoke. In short, the play you have at hand was meant for the stage, not for the page.

- Shakespeare had the same love of reforming and rearranging words in such places as hip-hop and sportscasting today. His plays reflect an excitement about language and an inventiveness that becomes enjoyable once the reader gets into the spirit of it.

- Since Shakespeare puts all types of people on stage, those characters will include some who are pompous, some who are devious, some who are boring, and some who are crazy, and all of these will speak in ways that are sometimes trying. Modern playwrights creating similar characters have them speak in similarly challenging ways.

12. Stage Directions:

Shakespeare's stagecraft went hand-in-hand with his wordcraft. For that reason, we believe it is important for the reader to know which stage directions are modern and which derive from Shakespeare's earliest text—the single-play Quartos or the Folio, the first collected works (1623). All stage directions appear in italics, but the brackets enclose modern additions to the stage directions. Readers may assume that the unbracketed stage directions appear in the Quarto and/or Folio versions of the play.

13. Scene Locations:

Shakespeare imagined his plays, first and foremost, on the stage of his outdoor or indoor theatre. The original printed versions of the plays do not give imaginary scene locations, except when they are occasionally mentioned in the dialogue. As an aid to the reader, this edition does include scene locations at the beginning of each scene, but puts all such locations in brackets to remind the reader that *this is not what Shakespeare envisioned and only possibly what he imagined.*

Reading Pointers for Sharper Insights

Consider the following as you read *The Taming of the Shrew*:

Gender Roles—Some critics have seen this play as a sexist critique of women who were gaining too much power (the ruler of England, of course, was a woman). Others believe that Kate's final speech is ironic, and that she has found a way to rule her husband while appearing to be ruled.

Induction, Plot and Subplot—*The Taming of the Shrew* begins with an *Induction* (a brief prologue).

The play that follows interweaves a main plot—Petruchio's "taming" of Kate—with a subplot involving the schemes of Bianca's suitors-turned-tutors. The characters of the Induction do not appear in the play itself.

Try to trace the main and subordinate plots. Where do they branch off, and where do they come together? How does Shakespeare build up to major events in the play, and how does he conclude the action?

Also, look for a thematic connection between the Induction and the main play. It may help you to know that some critics believe part of the play has been lost, and the Induction actually is concluded in Act V; others see the play as complete without a return to the Induction. What do you think?

Contemporary and Classical Models—This is one of Shakespeare's early comedies. It, therefore, takes elements from other authors' plays. The model for *The Taming of the Shrew* was the Italian farce, itself based on Greek and Roman comedies by authors such as Plautus and Terence. These comedies usually contained common and predictable plot devices and stock characters.

In the play, Bianca's suitors arrange an elaborate system of disguises in order to gain access to her. Ancient comedies also often revolve around people in disguise, identical twins who are unaware of one another (and therefore confuse the other characters without meaning to), and other, similar plot devices.

Likewise, the following characters would have been immediately recognizable to the classical audience:

- a crafty slave orchestrating the "disguise" plot for his own gain;
- a girl of marriageable age;
- at least one suitor to the girl;
- a guardian or parent of the girl, who is tricked by the suitor(s), the slave, the girl, or some combination of the three.

How does Shakespeare change these characters and plot devices? Are the roles of some characters reduced or enlarged?

CHRISTOPHER SLY, a beggar
HOSTESS, PAGE, PLAYERS, HUNTSMEN, and SERVANTS.
A Lord.

LUCENTIO, son to Vincentio

TRANIO } servant to Lucentio.

BAPTISTA, a rich gentleman of Padua.

KATHARINA, the shrew
BIANCA } daughters to Baptista.

GREMIO
HORTENSIO } suitors to Bianca.

BIONDELLO } servant to Lucentio.

PETRUCHIO, a gentleman of Verona, a suitor to Katharina.

GRUMIO
CURTIS } servants to Petruchio.

Servants attending Petruchio

TAILOR
HABERDASHER

A PEDANT (TEACHER)

VINCENTIO, an old gentleman of Pisa.

WIDOW

SCENE: Padua, and Petruchio's country house.

INDUCTION
SCENE I
[Before an alehouse on a heath.]

Enter beggar [Christopher Sly] and Hostess.

SLY: I'll pheeze[1] you, in faith.

HOS: A pair of stocks,[2] you rogue!

SLY: Ye are a baggage:[3] the Slys are no rogues; look in
the chronicles;[4] we came in with Richard[5] Conqueror.†

5 Therefore paucas[6] pallabris; let the world slide: sessa![7]

HOS: You will not pay for the glasses you have burst?

SLY: No, not a denier.[8] Go by, St. Jeronimy:[9] go to thy cold
bed, and warm thee.

HOS: I know my remedy; I must go fetch the third-borough.[10]

[Exit.]

10 SLY: Third, or fourth, or fifth borough, I'll answer him by
law: I'll not budge an inch, boy: let him come, and
kindly.   *Falls asleep.*

[Horns winded. Enter a Lord from hunting, with his train.]

LOR: Huntsman, I charge thee, tender[11] well my hounds:
15 Brach[12] Merriman, the poor cur is emboss'd;[13]
And couple Clowder with the deep-mouth'd brach.[14]
Saw'st thou not, boy, how Silver made it good
At the hedge-corner, in the coldest fault[15]?
I would not lose the dog for twenty pound.

20 HUN: Why, Belman is as good as he, my lord;
He cried upon it at the merest[16] loss
And twice to-day pick'd out the dullest scent:
Trust me, I take him for the better dog.

LOR: Thou art a fool: if Echo were as fleet,
25 I would esteem him worth a dozen such.
But sup them well and look unto them all:
To-morrow I intend to hunt again.

[1]*fix*

[2]*a device for punishment*†

[3]*worthless person*

[4]*recorded histories*

[5]*Sly's mistake for William the Conqueror*

[6]*Sly's version of pocas palabras, Spanish for "few words"*

[7]*French cessez, "cease"*

[8]*a French coin of little value*

[9]*St. Jerome*†

[10]*night policeman*

[11]*take care of*

[12]*rest*

[13]*foaming at the mouth from exhaustion*

[14]*a female hound*

[15]*loss of scent*

[16]*total*

†Terms marked in the text with (†) can be looked up in the Glossary for additional
information.

HUN: I will, my lord.

LOR: What's here? one dead, or drunk? See, doth he
30   breathe?

2ND HUN: He breathes, my lord. Were he not warm'd with ale,

This were a bed but cold to sleep so soundly.

LOR: O monstrous beast! how like a swine he lies!
35   Grim death, how foul and loathsome is thine image!

Sirs, I will practise on this drunken man.

What think you, if he were convey'd to bed,

Wrapp'd in sweet clothes, rings put upon his fingers,

A most delicious banquet by his bed,
40   And brave attendants near him when he wakes,

Would not the beggar then forget himself?

HUN: Believe me, lord, I think he cannot choose.

2ND HUN: It would seem strange unto him when he waked.

LOR: Even as a flattering dream or worthless fancy.
45   Then take him up and manage well the jest:

Carry him gently to my fairest chamber

And hang it round with all my wanton[17] pictures:

Balm his foul head in warm distilled waters

And burn sweet wood to make the lodging sweet:
50   Procure me music ready when he wakes,

To make a dulcet and a heavenly sound;

And if he chance to speak, be ready straight

And with a low submissive reverence

Say 'What is it your honour will command?'
55   Let one attend him with a silver basin

Full of rose-water and bestrew'd with flowers,

Another bear the ewer,[18] the third a diaper,[19]

And say 'Will't please your lordship cool your hands?'

Some one be ready with a costly suit
60   And ask him what apparel he will wear;

Another tell him of his hounds and horse,

And that his lady mourns at his disease:

Persuade him that he hath been lunatic;

And when he says he is, say that he dreams,
65   For he is nothing but a mighty lord.

This do and do it kindly, gentle sirs:

It will be pastime passing excellent,

If it be husbanded[20] with modesty.

[17]*erotic*

[18]*pitcher*

[19]*napkin*

[20]*handled*

HUN: My lord, I warrant you we will play our part,
70   As he shall think by our true diligence
      He is no less than what we say he is.
  LOR: Take him up gently and to bed with him;
      And each one to his office when he wakes.

                                    Sound trumpets.

      Sirrah, go see what trumpet 'tis that sounds:
75   Belike, some noble gentleman that means,
      Travelling some journey, to repose him here.

Enter Servingman.
      How now! who is it?
  SER: An't[21] please your honour, players
      That offer service to your lordship.

[21]*and it or if it*

[Enter Players.]
80 LOR: Bid them come near.
      Now, fellows, you are welcome.
  PLAYERS: We thank your honour.
  LOR: Do you intend to stay with me tonight?
  2ND PLAYER: So please your lordship to accept our duty.
85 LOR: With all my heart. This fellow I remember,
      Since once he play'd a farmer's eldest son:
      'Twas where you woo'd the gentlewoman so well:
      I have forgot your name; but, sure, that part
      Was aptly fitted and naturally perform'd.
90 A PLAYER: I think 'twas Soto that your honour means.
  LOR: 'Tis very true: thou didst it excellent.
      Well, you are come to me in happy time;
      The rather for I have some sport in hand
      Wherein your cunning can assist me much.
95   There is a lord will hear you play to-night:
      But I am doubtful of your modesties;
      Lest over-eyeing of his odd behavior,—
      For yet his honour never heard a play—
      You break into some merry passion
100   And so offend him; for I tell you, sirs,
      If you should smile he grows impatient.
  A PLAYER: Fear not, my lord: we can contain ourselves,
      Were he the veriest[22] antic[23] in the world.

[22]*most absolute*

[23]*fool*

²⁴a storehouse for
liquor

LOR: Go, sirrah, take them to the buttery,²⁴

105   And give them friendly welcome every one:
             Let them want nothing that my house affords.

                                                  Exit one with the Players.

             Sirrah, go you to Barthol'mew my page,
             And see him dress'd in all suits like a lady:

110   That done, conduct him to the drunkard's chamber;

²⁵slavish service

             And call him 'madam,' do him obeisance.²⁵
             Tell him from me, as he will win my love,
             He bear himself with honourable action,
             Such as he hath observed in noble ladies

115   Unto their lords, by them accomplished:
             Such duty to the drunkard let him do
             With soft low tongue and lowly courtesy,
             And say 'What is't your honour will command,
             Wherein your lady and your humble wife

120   May show her duty and make known her love?'
             And then with kind embracements, tempting kisses,
             And with declining head into his bosom,
             Bid him shed tears, as being overjoy'd
             To see her noble lord restored to health,

125   Who for this seven years hath esteem'd him
             No better than a poor and loathsome beggar:
             And if the boy have not a woman's gift
             To rain a shower of commanded tears,
             An onion will do well for such a shift,

130   Which in a napkin being close convey'd
             Shall in despite enforce a watery eye.
             See this dispatch'd with all the haste thou canst:
             Anon I'll give thee more instructions.

                                                  Exit a Servingman.

             I know the boy will well usurp the grace,

135   Voice, gait and action of a gentlewoman:
             I long to hear him call the drunkard husband,
             And how my men will stay themselves from laughter
             When they do homage to this simple peasant.
             I'll in to counsel them; haply my presence

140   May well abate the over-merry spleen
             Which otherwise would grow into extremes.

SCENE II
[A bedchamber in the Lord's house.]

Enter aloft the drunkard [Sly] with Attendants; some with apparel, Basin and Ewer, & appurtenances & Lord.

SLY: For God's sake, a pot of small ale.

1ST SER: Will't please your lordship drink a cup of sack?[26]

2ND SER: Will't please your honour taste of these conserves?[27]

3RD SER: What raiment[28] will your honour wear to-day?

5   SLY: I am Christophero Sly; call not me 'honour' nor 'lordship': I ne'er drank sack in my life; and if you give me
any conserves, give me conserves of beef: ne'er ask me
what raiment I'll wear; for I have no more doublets[29] than
backs, no more stockings than legs, nor no more shoes
10   than feet; nay, sometimes more feet than shoes, or such
shoes as my toes look through the over-leather.

LOR: Heaven cease this idle humour in your honour!
O, that a mighty man of such descent,
Of such possessions and so high esteem,
15   Should be infused with so foul a spirit!

SLY: What, would you make me mad? Am not I Christopher
Sly, old Sly's son of Burtonheath, by birth a pedlar,[30] by
education a cardmaker,[31] by transmutation[32] a bear-herd,[33]
and now by present profession a tinker?[34] Ask Marian
20   Hacket, the fat ale-wife of Wincot, if she know me not: if
she say I am not fourteen pence on the score[35] for sheer
ale, score me up for the lyingest knave in Christendom.
What! I am not bestraught:[36] here's—

3RD SER: O, this it is that makes your lady mourn!

2ND SER: O, this is it that makes your servants droop!

25   LOR: Hence comes it that your kindred shuns your house,
As beaten hence by your strange lunacy.
O noble lord, bethink thee of thy birth,
Call home thy ancient thoughts from banishment
And banish hence these abject lowly dreams.
30   Look how thy servants do attend on thee,
Each in his office ready at thy beck.
Wilt thou have music? hark! Apollo[37] plays,   *Music.*
And twenty caged nightingales do sing:

[26]*costly imported wine*

[27]*candied fruit*

[28]*garment*

[29]*jackets*

[30]*peddler*

[31]*a maker of cards for combing wool*

[32]*change of form*

[33]*a bear-tamer*

[34]*a mender of brass objects; also a word meaning "rascal" or "drunkard"*

[35]*Sly owes fourteen pence for beer.*

[36]*insane*

[37]*the Greek god of music*

[38]*a legendary queen of Assyria*†

[39]*decorated*

[40]*sky*

[41]*hunt*

[42]*swift*

[43]*deer*

[44]*a beautiful young man loved by Aphrodite*†

[45]*Aphrodite, goddess of love*

[46]*a young woman loved by Zeus*†

[47]*tricked*

[48]*a young woman pursued by Apollo*†

[49]*cheapest*

        Or wilt thou sleep? we'll have thee to a couch

35   Softer and sweeter than the lustful bed

        On purpose trimm'd up for Semiramis.[38]

        Say thou wilt walk; we will bestrew the ground:

        Or wilt thou ride? thy horses shall be trapp'd,[39]

        Their harness studded all with gold and pearl.

40   Dost thou love hawking? thou hast hawks will soar

        Above the morning lark: or wilt thou hunt?

        Thy hounds shall make the welkin[40] answer them

        And fetch shrill echoes from the hollow earth.

    1ST [SER]:   Say thou wilt course;[41] thy greyhounds are as swift

45   As breathed[42] stags, ay, fleeter than the roe.[43]

    2ND [SER]: Dost thou love pictures?† we will fetch thee straight

        Adonis[44] painted by a running brook,

        And Cytherea[45] all in sedges hid,

50   Which seem to move and wanton with her breath,

        Even as the waving sedges play with wind.

    LOR: We'll show thee Io[46] as she was a maid,

        And how she was beguiled[47] and surprised,

        As lively painted as the deed was done.

55   3RD [SER]:   Or Daphne[48] roaming through a thorny wood,

        Scratching her legs that one shall swear she bleeds,

        And at that sight shall sad Apollo weep,

        So workmanly the blood and tears are drawn.

    LOR: Thou art a lord, and nothing but a lord:

60   Thou hast a lady far more beautiful

        Than any woman in this waning age.

    1ST [SER]: And till the tears that she hath shed for thee

        Like envious floods o'er-run her lovely face,

        She was the fairest creature in the world;

65   And yet she is inferior to none.

    SLY: Am I a lord? and have I such a lady?

        Or do I dream? or have I dream'd till now?

        I do not sleep: I see, I hear, I speak;

        I smell sweet savours and I feel soft things:

70   Upon my life, I am a lord indeed

        And not a tinker nor Christophero Sly.

        Well, bring our lady hither to our sight;

        And once again, a pot o' the smallest[49] ale.

2ND [SER]:   Will't please your mightiness to wash your hands?
75   O, how we joy to see your wit restored!
        O, that once more you knew but what you are!
        These fifteen years you have been in a dream;
        Or when you waked, so waked as if you slept.
SLY: These fifteen years! by my fay,[50] a goodly nap.
80   But did I never speak of all that time?
1ST [SER]: O, yes, my lord, but very idle words:
        For though you lay here in this goodly chamber,
        Yet would you say ye were beaten out of door;
        And rail upon the hostess of the house;
85   And say you would present her at the leet,[51]
        Because she brought stone jugs[52] and no seal'd[53] quarts:
        Sometimes you would call out for Cicely Hacket.
SLY: Ay, the woman's maid of the house.
3RD [SER]: Why, sir, you know no house nor no such maid,
90   Nor no such men as you have reckon'd up,
        As Stephen Sly and old John Naps of Greece
        And Peter Turph and Henry Pimpernell
        And twenty more such names and men as these
        Which never were nor no man ever saw.
95 SLY: Now Lord be thanked for my good amends!
ALL: Amen.
SLY: I thank thee: thou shalt not lose by it.

Enter [Page as a] Lady, with Attendants.
PAGE: How fares my noble lord?
SLY: Marry, I fare well, for here is cheer enough.
100   Where is my wife?
PAGE: Here, noble lord: what is thy will with her?
SLY: Are you my wife and will not call me husband?
        My men should call me 'lord': I am your goodman.
PAGE: My husband and my lord, my lord and husband;
105   I am your wife in all obedience.
SLY: I know it well. What must I call her?
LOR: Madam.
SLY: Al'ce madam, or Joan madam?
LOR: 'Madam,' and nothing else: so lords call ladies.
110 SLY: Madam wife, they say that I have dream'd
        And slept above some fifteen year or more.

[50]*faith*

[51]*court*

[52]*unmarked jars signifying poor-quality liquor*

[53]*containers bearing an official seal of quality*

PAG: Ay, and the time seems thirty unto me,
      Being all this time abandon'd from your bed.
SLY: 'Tis much. Servants, leave me and her alone.
115   Madam, undress you and come now to bed.
PAG: Thrice noble lord, let me entreat of you
      To pardon me yet for a night or two,
      Or, if not so, until the sun be set:
      For your physicians have expressly charged,
120   In peril to incur your former malady,
      That I should yet absent me from your bed:
      I hope this reason stands for my excuse.

54a sexual pun

SLY: Ay, it stands[54] so that I may hardly tarry so long. But
      I would be loath to fall into my dreams again: I will
125   therefore tarry in despite of the flesh and the blood.

Enter a Messenger.

MESS: Your honour's players, hearing your amendment,
      Are come to play a pleasant comedy;
      For so your doctors hold it very meet,

55clotted up

      Seeing too much sadness hath congeal'd[55] your blood,
130   And melancholy is the nurse of frenzy:
      Therefore they thought it good you hear a play
      And frame your mind to mirth and merriment,
      Which bars a thousand harms and lengthens life.

56a mistake for "comedy"

SLY: Marry, I will, let them play it. Is not a comontie[56] a
135   Christmas gambold or a tumbling-trick?[57]

57frolic; light enter-tainment

PAG: No, my good lord; it is more pleasing stuff.
SLY: What, household stuff?
PAG: It is a kind of history.
SLY: Well, we'll see't. Come, madam wife, sit by my side
140   and let the world slip: we shall ne'er be younger.

[Flourish.]

ACT 1

SCENE I
[Padua. A public place.]

Flourish. Enter Lucentio, and his man Tranio.

LUC: Tranio, since for the great desire I had
    To see fair Padua,[1] nursery of arts,
    I am arrived for fruitful Lombardy,[2]
    The pleasant garden of great Italy;
5   And by my father's love and leave am arm'd
    With his good will and thy good company,
    My trusty servant, well approved in all,
    Here let us breathe and haply institute
    A course of learning and ingenious studies.
10   Pisa renown'd for grave citizens
    Gave me my being and my father first,
    A merchant of great traffic through the world,
    Vincentio come of Bentivolii.
    Vincentio's son, brought up in Florence,
15   It shall become to serve all hopes conceived,
    To deck his fortune with his virtuous deeds:
    And therefore, Tranio, for the time I study,
    Virtue and that part of philosophy
    Will I apply that treats of happiness
20   By virtue specially to be achieved.
    Tell me thy mind; for I have Pisa[3] left
    And am to Padua come, as he that leaves
    A shallow plash to plunge him in the deep
    And with satiety seeks to quench his thirst.
25 TRA: *Mi perdonato,*[4] gentle master mine,
    I am in all affected as yourself;
    Glad that you thus continue your resolve

[1] *a city in Northeast Italy, site of a famous university*

[2] *a region in the North of Italy*

[3] *Pisa and Florence are Italian cities famous for art and culture.*

[4] *"Pardon me"*

To suck the sweets of sweet philosophy.
Only, good master, while we do admire
30   This virtue and this moral discipline,
Let's be no stoics[5] nor no stocks, I pray;
Or so devote to Aristotle's[6] cheques
As Ovid[7] be an outcast quite abjured:
Balk logic with acquaintance that you have
35   And practise rhetoric in your common talk;
Music and poesy use to quicken you;
The mathematics and the metaphysics,
Fall to them as you find your stomach serves you;
No profit grows where is no pleasure ta'en:
40   In brief, sir, study what you most affect.
Luc: Gramercies,[8] Tranio, well dost thou advise.
If, Biondello, thou wert come ashore,
We could at once put us in readiness,
And take a lodging fit to entertain
45   Such friends as time in Padua shall beget.
But stay a while: what company is this?
Tra: Master, some show to welcome us to town.

Enter Baptista with his two daughters Katharina & Bianca,
Gremio, a pantaloon,† Hortensio, suitor to Bianca.

Bap: Gentlemen, importune me no farther,
For how I firmly am resolved you know;
50   That is, not bestow my youngest daughter
Before I have a husband for the elder:
If either of you both love Katharina,
Because I know you well and love you well,
Leave shall you have to court her at your pleasure.
55 Gre: *[Aside]* To cart[9] her rather: she's too rough for me.
There, there, Hortensio, will you any wife?
Kat: I pray you, sir, is it your will
To make a stale[10] of me amongst these mates?
Hor: Mates, maid! how mean you that? no mates for you,
60   Unless you were of gentler, milder mould.
Kat: I'faith, sir, you shall never need to fear:
I wis[11] it is not half way to her heart;
But if it were, doubt not her care should be

---

[5]*people who restrain their emotions†*

[6]*a Greek philosopher who stressed moderation*

[7]*a Roman love poet†*

[8]*Great thanks*

[9]*drive her in a cart†*

[10]*laughingstock; also a name for a prostitute*

[11]*surely*

	To comb your noddle[12] with a three-legg'd stool	[12]*head*
65	And paint your face and use you like a fool.	
	HOR: From all such devils, good Lord deliver us!	
	GRE: And me too, good Lord!	
	TRA: Hush, master! here's some good pastime toward:	
	That wench is stark mad or wonderful froward.[13]	[13]*stubborn, obstinate*
70	LUC: But in the other's silence do I see	
	Maid's mild behavior and sobriety.	
	Peace, Tranio!	
	TRA: Well said, master; mum! and gaze your fill.	
	BAP: Gentlemen, that I may soon make good	
75	What I have said, Bianca, get you in:	
	And let it not displease thee, good Bianca,	
	For I will love thee ne'er the less, my girl.	
	KAT: A pretty peat![14] it is best	[14]*pet*
	Put finger in the eye,[15] an she knew why.	[15]*i.e., cry*
80	BIA: Sister, content you in my discontent.	
	Sir, to your pleasure humbly I subscribe:	
	My books and instruments shall be my company,	
	On them to look and practise by myself.	
	LUC: Hark, Tranio! thou may'st hear Minerva[16] speak.	[16]*the Roman goddess of wisdom*†
85	HOR: Signior Baptista, will you be so strange?	
	Sorry am I that our good will effects	
	Bianca's grief.	
	GRE: Why will you mew[17] her up,	[17]*shut; also a coop (for caging a falcon)*
	Signior Baptista, for this fiend of hell,	
90	And make her[18] bear the penance of her tongue?	[18]*He points to Bianca and then to Kate.*
	BAP: Gentlemen, content ye; I am resolved:	
	Go in, Bianca: [*Exit.*]	
	And for I know she taketh most delight	
	In music, instruments and poetry,	
95	Schoolmasters will I keep within my house,	
	Fit to instruct her youth. If you, Hortensio,	
	Or Signior Gremio, you, know any such,	
	Prefer them hither; for to cunning men	
	I will be very kind, and liberal	
100	To mine own children in good bringing up.	
	And so farewell. Katharina, you may stay;	
	For I have more to commune with Bianca. *Exit.*	
	KAT: Why, and I trust I may go too, may I not?	

What, shall I be appointed hours; as though, belike, I
105   knew not what to take and what to leave, ha?   *Exit.*

GRE: You may go to the devil's dam:[19] your gifts are so
good, here's none will hold you. Their love is not so
great, Hortensio, but we may blow our nails together,[20]
and fast it fairly out: our cake's dough on both sides.[21]
110   Farewell: yet for the love I bear my sweet Bianca, if I
can by any means light on a fit man to teach her that
wherein she delights, I will wish him to her father.

HOR: So will I, Signior Gremio: but a word, I pray. Though
the nature of our quarrel yet never brooked[22] parle,[23]
115   know now, upon advice, it toucheth us both, that we
may yet again have access to our fair mistress and be
happy rivals in Bianca's love, to labour and effect one
thing specially.

GRE: What's that, I pray?

120 HOR: Marry, sir, to get a husband for her sister.

GRE: A husband! a devil.

HOR: I say, a husband.

GRE: I say, a devil. Thinkest thou, Hortensio, though her
father be very rich, any man is so very a fool to be mar-
125   ried to hell?

HOR: Tush, Gremio, though it pass your patience and mine
to endure her loud alarums, why, man, there be good
fellows in the world, an a man could light on them,
would take her with all faults, and money enough.

130 GRE: I cannot tell; but I had as lief[24] take her dowry with
this condition, to be whipped at the high cross every
morning.

HOR: Faith, as you say, there's small choice in rotten apples.
But come; since this bar in law makes us friends, it
135   shall be so far forth friendly maintained till by helping
Baptista's eldest daughter to a husband we set his youngest free for a husband, and then have to't afresh. Sweet
Bianca! Happy man be his dole![25] He that runs fastest
gets the ring. How say you, Signior Gremio?

140 GRE: I am agreed; and would I had given him the best
horse in Padua to begin his wooing that would thor-
oughly woo her, wed her and bed her and rid the house
of her! Come on.   *Exeunt [Gremio and Hortensio.]*
                                        Manet Tranio and Lucentio.

[19]*mother; mistress*

[20]*wait for some time*

[21]*i.e., the situation has not turned out as we hoped*

[22]*allowed for*

[23]*truce*

[24]*rather*

[25]*lot*

TRA: I pray, sir, tell me, is it possible

145   That love should of a sudden take such hold?

LUC: O Tranio, till I found it to be true,

I never thought it possible or likely;

But see, while idly I stood looking on,

I found the effect of love in idleness:

150   And now in plainness do confess to thee,

That art to me as secret and as dear

As Anna[26] to the queen of Carthage† was,

Tranio, I burn, I pine, I perish, Tranio,

If I achieve not this young modest girl.

155   Counsel me, Tranio, for I know thou canst;

Assist me, Tranio, for I know thou wilt.

TRA: Master, it is no time to chide you now;

Affection is not rated from the heart:

If love have touch'd you, nought remains but so,

160   'Redime te captum quam queas minimo.'[27]

LUC: Gramercies, lad, go forward; this contents:

The rest will comfort, for thy counsel's sound.

TRA: Master, you look'd so longly[28] on the maid,

Perhaps you mark'd not what's the pith of all.

165 LUC: O yes, I saw sweet beauty in her face,

Such as the daughter of Agenor[29] had,

That made great Jove to humble him to her hand,

When with his knees he kiss'd the Cretan† strand.

TRA: Saw you no more? mark'd you not how her sister

170   Began to scold and raise up such a storm

That mortal ears might hardly endure the din?

LUC: Tranio, I saw her coral lips to move

And with her breath she did perfume the air:

Sacred and sweet was all I saw in her.

175 TRA: Nay, then, 'tis time to stir him from his trance.

I pray, awake, sir: if you love the maid,

Bend thoughts and wits to achieve her. Thus it stands:

Her eldest sister is so curst and shrewd

That till the father rid his hands of her,

180   Master, your love must live a maid at home;

And therefore has he closely mew'd her up,

Because she will not be annoy'd with suitors.

LUC: Ah, Tranio, what a cruel father's he!

---

[26]*the sister of and confidante to Dido in the* Aeneid†

[27]*"Ransom yourself from captivity as cheaply as you can"†*

[28]*persistently*

[29]*Europa†*

  But art thou not advised, he took some care
185 To get her cunning schoolmasters to instruct her?
TRA: Ay, marry, am I, sir; and now 'tis plotted.
LUC: I have it, Tranio.
TRA: Master, for my hand,
  Both our inventions meet and jump in one.
190 LUC: Tell me thine first.
TRA: You will be schoolmaster
  And undertake the teaching of the maid:
  That's your device.
LUC: It is: may it be done?
195 TRA: Not possible; for who shall bear your part,
  And be in Padua here Vincentio's son,
  Keep house and ply his book, welcome his friends,
  Visit his countrymen and banquet them?
LUC: Basta;[30] content thee, for I have it full.
200 We have not yet been seen in any house,
  Nor can we lie distinguish'd by our faces
  For man or master; then it follows thus;
  Thou shalt be master, Tranio, in my stead,
  Keep house and port and servants as I should:
205 I will some other be, some Florentine,
  Some Neapolitan, or meaner[31] man of Pisa.
  'Tis hatch'd and shall be so: Tranio, at once
  Uncase[32] thee; take my colour'd hat and cloak:
  When Biondello comes, he waits on thee;
210 But I will charm him first to keep his tongue.
TRA: So had you need.
  In brief, sir, sith it your pleasure is,
  And I am tied to be obedient;
  For so your father charged me at our parting,
215 'Be serviceable to my son,' quoth he,
  Although I think 'twas in another sense;
  I am content to be Lucentio,
  Because so well I love Lucentio.
LUC: Tranio, be so, because Lucentio loves:
220 And let me be a slave, to achieve that maid
  Whose sudden sight hath thrall'd my wounded eye.
Enter Biondello.
  Here comes the rogue.

[30]*enough*

[31]*poorer*

[32]*undress*

Sirrah, where have you been?

BIO: Where have I been! Nay, how now! where are you?
225   Master, has my fellow Tranio stolen your clothes? Or you
stolen his? or both? Pray, what's the news?
LUC: Sirrah, come hither: 'tis no time to jest,
And therefore frame your manners to the time.
Your fellow Tranio here, to save my life,
230   Puts my apparel and my countenance on,
And I for my escape have put on his;
For in a quarrel since I came ashore
I kill'd a man and fear I was descried:[33]
Wait you on him, I charge you, as becomes,
235   While I make way from hence to save my life:
You understand me?
BIO: I, sir! ne'er a whit.
LUC: And not a jot of Tranio in your mouth:
Tranio is changed into Lucentio.
240 BIO: The better for him: would I were so too!
TRA: So could I, faith, boy, to have the next wish after,
That Lucentio indeed had Baptista's youngest daughter.
But, sirrah, not for my sake, but your master's, I advise
You use your manners discreetly in all kind of
245   companies:
When I am alone, why, then I am Tranio;
But in all places else your master Lucentio.
LUC: Tranio, let's go: one thing more rests, that thyself exe-
cute, to make one among these wooers: if thou ask me
250   why sufficeth my reasons are both good and weighty.

Exeunt.

The Presenters above speak.

1ST SER: My lord, you nod; you do not mind the play.
SLY: Yes, by Saint Anne, do I. A good matter, surely: comes
there any more of it?
255 PAG: My lord, 'tis but begun.
SLY: 'Tis a very excellent piece of work, madam lady: would
'twere done!   *They sit and mark.*

[33]*discovered*

SCENE II
[Padua. Before Hortensio's house.]

Enter Petruchio and his man Grumio.

PET: Verona, for a while I take my leave,
To see my friends in Padua, but of all
My best beloved and approved friend,
Hortensio; and I trow this is his house.
5   Here, sirrah Grumio; knock, I say.
GRU: Knock, sir! whom should I knock? is there man has
rebused[34] your worship?
PET: Villain, I say, knock me here soundly.[35]
GRU: Knock you here, sir! why, sir, what am I, sir, that I
10   should knock you here, sir?
PET: Villain, I say, knock me at this gate
And rap me well, or I'll knock your knave's pate.[36]
GRU: My master is grown quarrelsome. I should knock you
first, and then I know after who comes by the worst.
15 PET: Will it not be?
Faith, sirrah, an you'll not knock, I'll ring it;
I'll try how you can *Sol, Fa,* and sing it.
              He wrings him by the ears.
GRU: Help, masters, help! my master is mad.
PET: Now, knock when I bid you, sirrah villain!

Enter Hortensio.

20 HOR: How now! what's the matter? My old friend
Grumio! and my good friend Petruchio! How do you
all at Verona?
PET: Signior Hortensio, come you to part the fray?
'Con tutto il cuore, ben trovato,'[37] may I say.
25 HOR: 'Alla nostra casa ben venuto, molto honorato signor
mio Petruchio.'[38] Rise, Grumio, rise: we will compound[39] this quarrel.
GRU: Nay, 'tis no matter, sir, what he 'leges in Latin. If this
be not a lawful case for me to leave his service, look
30   you, sir, he bid me knock him and rap him soundly,
sir: well, was it fit for a servant to use his master so,

[34]*Grumio's mistake for "abused"*

[35]*both "loudly" (Petruchio's meaning) and "with great force" (Grumio's understanding)*

[36]*head*

[37]*"With my whole heart, welcome"*

[38]*"Welcome to our house, my most honored Sir Petruchio"*

[39]*settle*

being perhaps, for aught I see, two and thirty, a pip out?[40]

Whom would to God I had well knock'd at first, then had

not Grumio come by the worst.

35 PET: A senseless villain! Good Hortensio,

I bade the rascal knock upon your gate

And could not get him for my heart to do it.

GRU: Knock at the gate! O heavens! Spake you not these

words plain, 'Sirrah, knock me here, rap me here, knock

40 me well, and knock me soundly'? And come you now

with, 'knocking at the gate'?

PET: Sirrah, be gone, or talk not, I advise you.

HOR: Petruchio, patience; I am Grumio's pledge:[41]

Why, this's a heavy chance 'twixt him and you,

45 Your ancient, trusty, pleasant servant, Grumio.

And tell me now, sweet friend, what happy gale

Blows you to Padua here from old Verona?

PET: Such wind as scatters young men through the world,

To seek their fortunes farther than at home

50 Where small experience grows. But in a few,

Signior Hortensio, thus it stands with me:

Antonio, my father, is deceased;

And I have thrust myself into this maze,

Haply to wive and thrive as best I may:

55 Crowns in my purse I have and goods at home,

And so am come abroad to see the world.

HOR: Petruchio, shall I then come roundly[42] to thee

And wish thee to a shrewd ill-favour'd wife?

Thou'ldst[43] thank me but a little for my counsel:

60 And yet I'll promise thee she shall be rich

And very rich: but thou'rt too much my friend,

And I'll not wish thee to her.

PET: Signior Hortensio, 'twixt such friends as we

Few words suffice; and therefore, if thou know

65 One rich enough to be Petruchio's wife,

As wealth is burden of my wooing dance,

Be she as foul as was Florentius'[44] love,

As old as Sibyl[45] and as curst and shrewd

As Socrates' Xanthippe,[46] or a worse,

70 She moves me not, or not removes, at least,

Affection's edge in me, were she as rough

[40]*drunk*†

[41]*one who vouches for*

[42]*plainly*

[43]*you would*

[44]*a knight who married an ugly old woman*†

[45]*an ancient prophetess*†

[46]*the wife of the Greek philosopher Socrates, said to be bad-tempered*

[47]*sea between Italy and the Balkan peninsula*†

[48]*ornamental or a figure on a shoe-lace*

[49]*hag*

As are the swelling Adriatic[47] seas:
I come to wive it wealthily in Padua;
If wealthily, then happily in Padua.

75 GRU: Nay, look you, sir, he tells you flatly what his mind
is: why, give him gold enough and marry him to a puppet or an aglet-baby;[48] or an old trot[49] with ne'er a tooth
in her head, though she have as many diseases as two
and fifty horses: why, nothing comes amiss, so money
80   comes withal.

HOR: Petruchio, since we are stepp'd thus far in,
I will continue that I broach'd in jest.
I can, Petruchio, help thee to a wife
With wealth enough and young and beauteous,
85   Brought up as best becomes a gentlewoman:
Her only fault, and that is faults enough,
Is that she is intolerable curst
And shrewd and froward, so beyond all measure
That, were my state far worser than it is,
90   I would not wed her for a mine of gold.

PET: Hortensio, peace! thou know'st not gold's effect:
Tell me her father's name and 'tis enough;
For I will board her, though she chide as loud
As thunder when the clouds in autumn crack.

95 HOR: Her father is Baptista Minola,
An affable and courteous gentleman:
Her name is Katharina Minola,
Renown'd in Padua for her scolding tongue.

PET: I know her father, though I know not her;
100   And he knew my deceased father well.
I will not sleep, Hortensio, till I see her;
And therefore let me be thus bold with you
To give you over at this first encounter,
Unless you will accompany me thither.

105 GRU: I pray you, sir, let him go while the humour lasts. O'
my word, an she knew him as well as I do, she would
think scolding would do little good upon him: she may
perhaps call him half a score knaves or so: why, that's
nothing; an he begin once, he'll rail in his rope-tricks.[50]
110   I'll tell you what sir, an she stand him but a little, he
will throw a figure[51] in her face and so disfigure her

[50]*possibly a mistake for "rhetoric"*

[51]*figure of speech*

with it that she shall have no more eyes to see withal
than a cat. You know him not, sir.

Hor: Tarry,[52] Petruchio, I must go with thee,

115   For in Baptista's keep my treasure is:
He hath the jewel of my life in hold,
His youngest daughter, beautiful Bianca,
And her withholds from me and other more,
Suitors to her and rivals in my love,

120   Supposing it a thing impossible,
For those defects I have before rehearsed,
That ever Katharina will be woo'd;
Therefore this order hath Baptista ta'en,
That none shall have access unto Bianca

125   Till Katharina the curst have got a husband.

Gru: Katharina the curst!
A title for a maid of all titles the worst.

Hor: Now shall my friend Petruchio do me grace,
And offer me disguised in sober robes

130   To old Baptista as a schoolmaster
Well seen in music, to instruct Bianca;
That so I may, by this device, at least
Have leave and leisure to make love to her
And unsuspected court her by herself.

135 Gru: Here's no knavery! See, to beguile the old folks, how
the young folks lay their heads together!

Enter Gremio and Lucentio, disguised [as Cambio.]
Master, master, look about you: who goes there, ha?

Hor: Peace, Grumio! it is the rival of my love.
Petruchio, stand by a while.

140 Gru: A proper stripling[53] and an amorous!

Gre: O, very well; I have perused the note.
Hark you, sir: I'll have them very fairly bound:
All books of love, see that at any hand;
And see you read no other lectures to her:

145   You understand me: over and beside
Signior Baptista's liberality,
I'll mend it with a largess.[54] Take your paper too,
And let me have them very well perfumed

[52]*wait*

[53]*youngster*

[54]*generous gift*

For she is sweeter than perfume itself
150　　To whom they go to. What will you read to her?
LUC:　Whate'er I read to her, I'll plead for you
As for my patron, stand you so assured,
As firmly as yourself were still in place:
Yea, and perhaps with more successful words
155　　Than you, unless you were a scholar, sir.
GRE:　O this learning, what a thing it is!
GRU:　O this woodcock,[55] what an ass it is!
PET:　Peace, sirrah!
HOR:　Grumio, mum! God save you, Signior Gremio.
160　GRE:　And you are well met, Signior Hortensio.
Trow[56] you whither I am going? To Baptista Minola.
I promised to inquire carefully
About a schoolmaster for the fair Bianca:
And by good fortune I have lighted well
165　　On this young man, for learning and behavior
Fit for her turn, well read in poetry
And other books, good ones, I warrant ye.
HOR:　'Tis well; and I have met a gentleman
Hath promised me to help me to another,
170　　A fine musician to instruct our mistress;
So shall I no whit be behind in duty
To fair Bianca, so beloved of me.
GRE:　Beloved of me; and that my deeds shall prove.
GRU:　And that his bags shall prove.
175　HOR:　Gremio, 'tis now no time to vent our love:
Listen to me, and if you speak me fair,
I'll tell you news indifferent good for either.
Here is a gentleman whom by chance I met,
Upon agreement from us to his liking,
180　　Will undertake to woo curst Katharina,
Yea, and to marry her, if her dowry please.
GRE:　So said, so done, is well.
Hortensio, have you told him all her faults?
PET:　I know she is an irksome brawling scold:
185　　If that be all, masters, I hear no harm.
GRE:　No, say'st me so, friend? What countryman?
PET:　Born in Verona, old Antonio's son:
My father dead, my fortune lives for me;
And I do hope good days and long to see.

190 GRE: O sir, such a life, with such a wife, were strange!
         But if you have a stomach, to't i' God's name:
         You shall have me assisting you in all.
         But will you woo this wild-cat?
  PET: Will I live?
195 GRU: Will he woo her? ay, or I'll hang her.
  PET: Why came I hither but to that intent?
         Think you a little din can daunt mine ears?
         Have I not in my time heard lions roar?
         Have I not heard the sea puff'd up with winds
200   Rage like an angry boar chafed with sweat?
         Have I not heard great ordnance[57] in the field,
         And heaven's artillery thunder in the skies?
         Have I not in a pitched battle heard
         Loud 'larums, neighing steeds, and trumpets' clang?
205   And do you tell me of a woman's tongue,
         That gives not half so great a blow to hear
         As will a chestnut in a farmer's fire?
         Tush, tush! fear boys with bugs.
  GRU: For he fears none.
210 GRE: Hortensio, hark:
         This gentleman is happily arrived,
         My mind presumes, for his own good and ours.
  HOR: I promised we would be contributors
         And bear his charge of wooing, whatsoe'er.
215 GRE: And so we will, provided that he win her.
  GRU: I would I were as sure of a good dinner.

Enter Tranio brave, and Biondello.

  TRA: Gentlemen, God save you. If I may be bold,
         Tell me, I beseech you, which is the readiest way
         To the house of Signior Baptista Minola?
220 BIO: He that has the two fair daughters: is't he you mean?
  TRA: Even he, Biondello.
  GRE: Hark you, sir; you mean not her to—
  TRA: Perhaps, him and her, sir: what have you to do?
  PET: Not her that chides, sir, at any hand, I pray.
225 TRA: I love no chiders, sir. Biondello, let's away.
  LUC: Well begun, Tranio.

[57] *artillery*

[58]before

HOR: Sir, a word ere[58] you go;

    Are you a suitor to the maid you talk of, yea or no?

TRA: And if I be, sir, is it any offence?

230 GRE: No; if without more words you will get you hence.

TRA: Why, sir, I pray, are not the streets as free

    For me as for you?

GRE: But so is not she.

TRA: For what reason, I beseech you?

235 GRE: For this reason, if you'll know,

    That she's the choice love of Signior Gremio.

HOR: That she's the chosen of Signior Hortensio.

TRA: Softly, my masters! if you be gentlemen,

    Do me this right; hear me with patience.

240   Baptista is a noble gentleman,

    To whom my father is not all unknown;

    And were his daughter fairer than she is,

    She may more suitors have and me for one.

    Fair Leda's daughter had a thousand wooers;

245   Then well one more may fair Bianca have:

    And so she shall; Lucentio shall make one,

    Though Paris came in hope to speed alone.

GRE: What! this gentleman will out-talk us all.

[59]a worn-out horse or worthless fellow†

LUC: Sir, give him head: I know he'll prove a jade.[59]

250 PET: Hortensio, to what end are all these words?

HOR: Sir, let me be so bold as ask you,

    Did you yet ever see Baptista's daughter?

TRA: No, sir; but hear I do that he hath two,

    The one as famous for a scolding tongue

255   As is the other for beauteous modesty.

PET: Sir, sir, the first's for me; let her go by.

GRE: Yea, leave that labour to great Hercules;[60]

    And let it be more than Alcides' twelve.

[60]in classical mythology, the strongest man in the world†

PET: Sir, understand you this of me in sooth:

260   The youngest daughter whom you hearken for

    Her father keeps from all access of suitors,

    And will not promise her to any man

    Until the elder sister first be wed:

    The younger then is free and not before.

265 TRA: If it be so, sir, that you are the man

    Must stead us all and me amongst the rest,

And if you break the ice and do this feat,
Achieve the elder, set the younger free
For our access, whose hap shall be to have her
270　Will not so graceless be to be ingrate.
　HOR:　Sir, you say well and well you do conceive;
And since you do profess to be a suitor,
You must, as we do, gratify this gentleman,
To whom we all rest generally beholding.
275　TRA:　Sir, I shall not be slack: in sign whereof,
Please ye we may contrive this afternoon,
And quaff[61] carouses[62] to our mistress' health, 　　[61]*drink*
And do as adversaries do in law, 　　[62]*toasts*
Strive mightily, but eat and drink as friends.
280　GRU, BIO:　O excellent motion! Fellows, let's be gone.
　HOR:　The motion's good indeed and be it so,
Petruchio, I shall be your ben venuto.[63] 　　[63]*welcome*

Exeunt.

[ACT II]

[SCENE I]
[Padua. A room in Baptista's house.]

Enter Katharina and Bianca.

BIA: Good sister, wrong me not, nor wrong yourself,
    To make a bondmaid and a slave of me;
    That I disdain: but for these other goods,[1]
    Unbind my hands, I'll pull them off myself,
5   Yea, all my raiment,[2] to my petticoat;
    Or what you will command me will I do,
    So well I know my duty to my elders.
KAT: Of all thy suitors, here I charge thee, tell
    Whom thou lovest best: see thou dissemble not.
10 BIA: Believe me, sister, of all the men alive
    I never yet beheld that special face
    Which I could fancy more than any other.
KAT: Minion, thou liest. Is't not Hortensio?
BIA: If you affect him, sister, here I swear
15   I'll plead for you myself, but you shall have him.
KAT: O then, belike, you fancy riches more:
    You will have Gremio to keep you fair.
BIA: Is it for him you do envy me so?
    Nay then you jest, and now I well perceive
20   You have but jested with me all this while:
    I prithee, sister Kate, untie my hands.
KAT: If that be jest, then all the rest was so.   *Strikes her.*

Enter Baptista.

BAP: Why, how now, dame! whence grows this insolence?
    Bianca, stand aside. Poor girl! she weeps.

[1]*trinkets*

[2]*clothing*

37

25   Go ply thy needle; meddle not with her.

        For shame, thou hilding³ of a devilish spirit,
        Why dost thou wrong her that did ne'er wrong thee?
        When did she cross thee with a bitter word?

KAT: Her silence flouts me, and I'll be revenged.

                                    Flies after Bianca.

30 BAP: What, in my sight? Bianca, get thee in.

                                    Exit Bianca.

KAT: What, will you not suffer me? Nay, now I see
        She is your treasure, she must have a husband;
        I must dance bare-foot⁴ on her wedding day

        And for your love to her lead apes in hell.
35   Talk not to me: I will go sit and weep
        Till I can find occasion of revenge.

BAP: Was ever gentleman thus grieved as I?
        But who comes here?

*[Enter Gremio, Lucentio, in the habit of a mean man, Petruchio
with Tranio, with his boy [Biondello] bearing a Lute and Books,
and Hortensio as a musician.]*

GRE: Good morrow, neighbour Baptista.
40 BAP: Good morrow, neighbour Gremio.
        God save you, gentlemen!
PET: And you, good sir! Pray, have you not a daughter
        Call'd Katharina, fair and virtuous?
BAP: I have a daughter, sir, called Katharina.
45 GRE: You are too blunt: go to it orderly.
PET: You wrong me, Signior Gremio: give me leave.
        I am a gentleman of Verona, sir,
        That, hearing of her beauty and her wit,
        Her affability and bashful modesty,
50   Her wondrous qualities and mild behavior,
        Am bold to show myself a forward guest
        Within your house, to make mine eye the witness
        Of that report which I so oft have heard.
        And, for an entrance to my entertainment,
55   I do present you with a man of mine,
        Cunning in music and the mathematics,

To instruct her fully in those sciences,
Whereof I know she is not ignorant:
Accept of him, or else you do me wrong:

60 His name is Licio, born in Mantua.⁵

BAP: You're welcome, sir; and he, for your good sake.
But for my daughter Katharina, this I know,
She is not for your turn, the more my grief.

PET: I see you do not mean to part with her,

65 Or else you like not of my company.

BAP: Mistake me not; I speak but as I find.
Whence are you, sir? what may I call your name?

PET: Petruchio is my name; Antonio's son,
A man well known throughout all Italy.

70 BAP: I know him well: you are welcome for his sake.

GRE: Saving your tale, Petruchio, I pray,
Let us, that are poor petitioners, speak too:
Backare!⁶ you are marvellous forward.

PET: O, pardon me, Signior Gremio; I would fain⁷ be doing.

75 GRE: I doubt it not, sir; but you will curse your wooing.
Neighbour, this is a gift very grateful, I am sure of it.
To express the like kindness, myself, that have been
more kindly beholding to you than any, freely give unto
you this young scholar, that hath been long studying at

80 Rheims;⁸ as cunning in Greek, Latin, and other languag-
es, as the other in music and mathematics: his name is
Cambio; pray, accept his service.

BAP: A thousand thanks, Signior Gremio.
Welcome, good Cambio.

85 But, gentle sir, methinks you walk like a stranger: may I
be so bold to know the cause of your coming?

TRA: Pardon me, sir, the boldness is mine own,
That, being a stranger in this city here,
Do make myself a suitor to your daughter,

90 Unto Bianca, fair and virtuous.
Nor is your firm resolve unknown to me,
In the preferment of the eldest sister.
This liberty is all that I request,
That, upon knowledge of my parentage,

95 I may have welcome 'mongst the rest that woo
And free access and favour as the rest:

⁵*a city in Northern Italy*

⁶*stay back [false Latin]*

⁷*gladly*

⁸*a city in northeastern France; site of a famous university*

And, toward the education of your daughters,
I here bestow a simple instrument,
And this small packet of Greek and Latin books:
100   If you accept them, then their worth is great.
BAP: Lucentio is your name; of whence, I pray?
TRA: Of Pisa, sir; son to Vincentio.
BAP: A mighty man of Pisa; by report
I know him well: you are very welcome, sir.
105   Take you the lute, and you the set of books;
You shall go see your pupils presently.
Holla, within!

Enter a Servant.
Sirrah, lead these gentlemen
To my daughters; and tell them both,
110   These are their tutors: bid them use them well.
        [Exit Servant, with Lucentio and Hortensio, Biondello
        following.]
We will go walk a little in the orchard,
And then to dinner. You are passing welcome,
And so I pray you all to think yourselves.
PET: Signior Baptista, my business asketh haste,
115   And every day I cannot come to woo.
You knew my father well, and in him me,
Left solely heir to all his lands and goods,
Which I have better'd rather than decreased:
Then tell me, if I get your daughter's love,
120   What dowry shall I have with her to wife?
BAP: After my death the one half of my lands,
And in possession twenty thousand crowns.
PET: And, for that dowry, I'll assure her of
Her widowhood, be it that she survive me,
125   In all my lands and leases whatsoever:
Let specialties⁹ be therefore drawn between us,
That covenants may be kept on either hand.
BAP: Ay, when the special thing is well obtain'd,
That is, her love; for that is all in all.
130 PET: Why, that is nothing: for I tell you, father,
I am as peremptory¹⁰ as she proud-minded;
And where two raging fires meet together

⁹*contracts*

¹⁰*determined*

They do consume the thing that feeds their fury:
Though little fire grows great with little wind,
135 Yet extreme gusts will blow out fire and all:
So I to her and so she yields to me;
For I am rough and woo not like a babe.
BAP: Well mayst thou woo, and happy be thy speed!
But be thou arm'd for some unhappy words.
140 PET: Ay, to the proof;[11] as mountains are for winds,
That shake not, though they blow perpetually.
Enter Hortensio, with his head broke.
BAP: How now, my friend! why dost thou look so pale?
HOR: For fear, I promise you, if I look pale.
BAP: What, will my daughter prove a good musician?
145 HOR: I think she'll sooner prove a soldier.
Iron may hold with her, but never lutes.
BAP: Why, then thou canst not break her to the lute?
HOR: Why, no; for she hath broke the lute to me.
I did but tell her she mistook her frets,[12]
150 And bow'd her hand to teach her fingering;
When, with a most impatient devilish spirit,
'Frets, call you these?' quoth she; 'I'll fume[13] with them:'†
And, with that word, she struck me on the head,
And through the instrument my pate made way;
155 And there I stood amazed for a while,
As on a pillory,[14] looking through the lute;
While she did call me rascal fiddler
And twangling Jack; with twenty such vile terms,
As had she studied to misuse me so.
160 PET: Now, by the world, it is a lusty wench;
I love her ten times more than e'er I did:
O, how I long to have some chat with her!
BAP: Well, go with me and be not so discomfited:
Proceed in practise with my younger daughter;
165 She's apt to learn and thankful for good turns.
Signior Petruchio, will you go with us,
Or shall I send my daughter Kate to you?
PET: I pray you do.   *Exit Manet Petruchio.*
I will attend her here,
170 And woo her with some spirit when she comes.
Say that she rail; why then I'll tell her plain

[11]*point that I will succeed*

[12]*markers on an instrument*

[13]*rage*

[14]*stocks*

She sings as sweetly as a nightingale:
Say that she frown, I'll say she looks as clear
As morning roses newly wash'd with dew:
175 Say she be mute and will not speak a word;
Then I'll commend her volubility,
And say she uttereth piercing eloquence:
If she do bid me pack, I'll give her thanks,
As though she bid me stay by her a week:
180 If she deny to wed, I'll crave the day
When I shall ask the banns[15] and when be married.
But here she comes; and now, Petruchio, speak.

Enter Katharina.

Good morrow, Kate; for that's your name, I hear.
KAT: Well have you heard, but something hard of hearing:
185   They call me Katharina that do talk of me.
PET: You lie, in faith; for you are call'd plain Kate,
And bonny Kate and sometimes Kate the curst;
But Kate, the prettiest Kate in Christendom,[16]
Kate of Kate-hall, my super-dainty Kate,
190   For dainties are all Kates, and therefore, Kate,
Take this of me, Kate of my consolation;
Hearing thy mildness praised in every town,
Thy virtues spoke of, and thy beauty sounded,
Yet not so deeply as to thee belongs,
195   Myself am moved to woo thee for my wife.
KAT: Moved! in good time: let him that moved you hither
Remove you hence: I knew you at the first
You were a moveable.
PET: Why, what's a moveable?
200 KAT: A join'd-stool.[17]
PET: Thou hast hit it: come, sit on me.
KAT: Asses are made to bear, and so are you.
PET: Women are made to bear,[18] and so are you.
KAT: No such jade as you, if me you mean.
205 PET: Alas! good Kate, I will not burden thee;
For, knowing thee to be but young and light—
KAT: Too light for such a swain[19] as you to catch;
And yet as heavy as my weight should be.
PET: Should be! should—buzz![20]
210 KAT: Well ta'en, and like a buzzard.

[15]*declare my intention to marry in church*†

[16]*the Christian world*

[17]*a proverbial term for a fool; idiot*

[18]*He puns on "bear," meaning "to bear children."*

[19]*country boy*

[20]*He plays on the word "be," making a noise like a bee.*

PET: O slow-wing'd turtle![21] shall a buzzard take thee?

KAT: Ay, for a turtle, as he takes a buzzard.

PET: Come, come, you wasp; i' faith, you are too angry.

KAT: If I be waspish, best beware my sting.

215 PET: My remedy is then, to pluck it out.

KAT: Ay, if the fool could find it where it lies,

PET: Who knows not where a wasp does wear his sting? In
     his tail.

KAT: In his tongue.

220 PET: Whose tongue?

KAT: Yours, if you talk of tails: and so farewell.

PET: What, with my tongue in your tail? nay, come again,
     Good Kate; I am a gentleman.

KAT: That I'll try.   *She strikes him.*

225 PET: I swear I'll cuff you, if you strike again.

KAT: So may you lose your arms:[22]
     If you strike me, you are no gentleman;
     And if no gentleman, why then no arms.

PET: A herald,† Kate? O, put me in thy books!

230 KAT: What is your crest?[23] a coxcomb?

PET: A combless cock, so Kate will be my hen.

KAT: No cock of mine; you crow too like a craven.[24]

PET: Nay, come, Kate, come; you must not look so sour.

KAT: It is my fashion, when I see a crab.

235 PET: Why, here's no crab; and therefore look not sour.

KAT: There is, there is.

PET: Then show it me.

KAT: Had I a glass, I would.

PET: What, you mean my face?

240 KAT: Well aim'd of such a young one.

PET: Now, by Saint George, I am too young for you.

KAT: Yet you are wither'd.

PET: 'Tis with cares.

KAT: I care not.

245 PET: Nay, hear you, Kate: in sooth you scape not so.

KAT: I chafe[25] you, if I tarry: let me go.

PET: No, not a whit: I find you passing gentle.
     'Twas told me you were rough and coy and sullen,
     And now I find report a very liar;

250   For thou are pleasant, gamesome, passing courteous,
     But slow in speech, yet sweet as spring-time flowers:

[21]*turtledove*

[22]*both "limbs" and "coat of arms, family crest"*

[23]*a play on "crest" (picture on a coat of arms) and "crest" (hair or feathers on the head, also called a "comb"; a cox- comb is a fool)*

[24]*a cowardly roost- er, one that will not fight*

[25]*irritate*

Thou canst not frown, thou canst not look askance,
Nor bite the lip, as angry wenches will,
Nor hast thou pleasure to be cross in talk,
255   But thou with mildness entertain'st thy wooers,
With gentle conference, soft and affable.
Why does the world report that Kate doth limp?
O slanderous world! Kate like the hazel-twig
Is straight and slender and as brown in hue
260   As hazel nuts and sweeter than the kernels.
O, let me see thee walk: thou dost not halt.[26]

KAT: Go, fool, and whom thou keep'st[27] command.

PET: Did ever Dian so become a grove
As Kate this chamber with her princely gait?
265   O, be thou Dian,[28] and let her be Kate;
And then let Kate be chaste and Dian† sportful!

KAT: Where did you study all this goodly speech?

PET: It is extempore,[29] from my mother-wit.

KAT: A witty mother! witless else her son.

270 PET: Am I not wise?

KAT: Yes; keep you warm.[30]

PET: Marry,[31] so I mean, sweet Katharina, in thy bed:
And therefore, setting all this chat aside,
Thus in plain terms: your father hath consented
275   That you shall be my wife; your dowry 'greed on;
And, will you, nill you, I will marry you.
Now, Kate, I am a husband for your turn;
For, by this light, whereby I see thy beauty,
Thy beauty, that doth make me like thee well,
280   Thou must be married to no man but me;

Enter Baptista, Gremio, Tranio.
For I am he am born to tame you, Kate,
And bring you from a wild Kate to a Kate
Conformable as other household Kates.
Here comes your father: never make denial;
285   I must and will have Katharina to my wife.

BAP: Now, Signior Petruchio, how speed[32] you with my
daughter?

[26]*limp*

[27]*i.e., your servants*

[28]*Diana, the Greek goddess of chastity and the hunt*

[29]*improvised*

[30]*i.e., you have enough wisdom to keep you warm [proverbial saying]*

[31]*by the Virgin Mary, an oath*

[32]*succeed*

PET: How but well, sir? how but well?
　　It were impossible I should speed amiss.
290 BAP:　Why, how now, daughter Katharina! in your dumps?
　　KAT:　Call you me daughter? now, I promise you
　　　　You have show'd a tender fatherly regard,
　　　　To wish me wed to one half lunatic;
　　　　A mad-cup ruffian and a swearing Jack,
295　　　That thinks with oaths to face[33] the matter out.
　　PET: Father, 'tis thus: yourself and all the world,
　　　　That talk'd of her, have talk'd amiss of her:
　　　　If she be curst, it is for policy,[34]
　　　　For she's not froward, but modest as the dove;
300　　　She is not hot, but temperate as the morn;
　　　　For patience she will prove a second Grissel,[35]
　　　　And Roman Lucrece[36] for her chastity:
　　　　And to conclude, we have 'greed so well together,
　　　　That upon Sunday is the wedding-day.
305 KAT:　I'll see thee hang'd on Sunday first.
　　GRE:　Hark, Petruchio; she says she'll see thee hang'd first.
　　TRA:　Is this your speeding? nay, then, good night our part!
　　PET: Be patient, gentlemen; I choose her for myself:
　　　　If she and I be pleased, what's that to you?
310　　　'Tis bargain'd 'twixt us twain,[37] being alone,
　　　　That she shall still be curst in company.
　　　　I tell you, 'tis incredible to believe
　　　　How much she loves me: O, the kindest Kate!
　　　　She hung about my neck; and kiss on kiss
315　　　She vied[38] so fast, protesting oath on oath,
　　　　That in a twink she won me to her love.
　　　　O, you are novices! 'Tis a world to see,
　　　　How tame, when men and women are alone,
　　　　A meacock[39] wretch can make the curstest shrew.
320　　　Give me thy hand, Kate: I will unto Venice,
　　　　To buy apparel 'gainst the wedding-day.
　　　　Provide the feast, father, and bid the guests;
　　　　I will be sure my Katharina shall be fine.
　　BAP:　I know not what to say: but give me your hands;
325　　　God send you joy, Petruchio! 'Tis a match.
　　GRE, TRA:　Amen, say we: we will be witnesses.

[33]*bluff*

[34]*show*

[35]*Griselda, a woman famed for patience*†

[36]*Lucretia, a Roman woman famous for her chastity*†

[37]*two*

[38]*raised the stakes*†

[39]*cowardly*

PET: Father, and wife, and gentlemen, adieu;

    I will to Venice; Sunday comes apace:[40]

    We will have rings and things and fine array;

330   And kiss me, Kate, we will be married o'Sunday.

                          Exit Petruchio and Katharina.

GRE: Was ever match clapp'd up so suddenly?

BAP: Faith, gentlemen, now I play a merchant's part,

    And venture madly on a desperate mart.[†]

TRA: 'Twas a commodity lay fretting[41] by you:

335   'Twill bring you gain, or perish on the seas.

BAP: The gain I seek is quiet in the match.[†]

GRE: No doubt but he hath got a quiet catch.

    But now, Baptista, to your younger daughter:

    Now is the day we long have looked for:

340   I am your neighbour, and was suitor first.

TRA: And I am one that love Bianca more

    Than words can witness, or your thoughts can guess.

GRE: Youngling, thou canst not love so dear as I.

TRA: Graybeard, thy love doth freeze.

345 GRE: But thine doth fry.

    Skipper, stand back: 'tis age that nourisheth.

TRA: But youth in ladies' eyes that flourisheth.

BAP: Content you, gentlemen: I will compound[42] this strife:

    'Tis deeds must win the prize; and he of both

350   That can assure my daughter greatest dower[43]

    Shall have my Bianca's love.

    Say, Signior Gremio, What can you assure her?

GRE: First, as you know, my house within the city

    Is richly furnished with plate and gold;

355   Basins and ewers to lave[44] her dainty hands;

    My hangings all of Tyrian[45] tapestry;

    In ivory coffers I have stuff'd my crowns;

    In cypress chests my arras[46] counterpoints,

    Costly apparel, tents, and canopies,

360   Fine linen, Turkey cushions boss'd[47] with pearl,

    Valance[48] of Venice gold in needlework,

    Pewter and brass and all things that belong

    To house or housekeeping: then, at my farm

    I have a hundred milch-kine[49] to the pail,

365   Sixscore fat oxen standing in my stalls,

---

[40]*quickly*

[41]*decaying*

[42]*settle*

[43]*dowry*

[44]*wash*

[45]*purple*[†]

[46]*a tapestry from Arras, in northern France*

[47]*embossed*

[48]*bed-curtain*

[49]*cows, dairy cattle*

And all things answerable to this portion.
Myself am struck in years, I must confess;
And if I die to-morrow, this is hers,
If whilst I live she will be only mine.
370   TRA: That 'only' came well in. Sir, list to me:
I am my father's heir and only son:
If I may have your daughter to my wife,
I'll leave her houses three or four as good,
Within rich Pisa walls, as any one
375 Old Signior Gremio has in Padua;
Besides two thousand ducats[50] by the year
Of fruitful land, all which shall be her jointure.[51]
What, have I pinch'd you, Signior Gremio?
  GRE: Two thousand ducats by the year of land!
380 My land amounts not to so much in all:
That she shall have; besides an argosy
That now is lying in Marseilles' road.
What, have I choked you with an argosy?[52]
  TRA: Gremio, 'tis known my father hath no less
385 Than three great argosies; besides two galliases,[53]
And twelve tight galleys: these I will assure her,
And twice as much, whate'er thou offer'st next.
  GRE: Nay, I have offer'd all, I have no more;
And she can have no more than all I have:
390 If you like me, she shall have me and mine.
  TRA: Why, then the maid is mine from all the world,
By your firm promise: Gremio is out-vied.
  BAP: I must confess your offer is the best;
And, let your father make her the assurance,
395 She is your own; else, you must pardon me,
if you should die before him, where's her dower?
  TRA: That's but a cavil:[54] he is old, I young.
  GRE: And may not young men die, as well as old?
  BAP: Well, gentlemen,
400 I am thus resolved: on Sunday next you know
My daughter Katharina is to be married:
Now, on the Sunday following, shall Bianca
Be bride to you, if you make this assurance;
If not, Signior Gremio:
405 And so, I take my leave, and thank you both.   *Exit.*

[50] *gold coins*

[51] *inheritance*

[52] *merchant-ship*

[53] *warships*

[54] *petty question*

GRE: Adieu, good neighbour.
      Now I fear thee not:
      Sirrah young gamester, your father were a fool
      To give thee all, and in his waning age
410   Set foot under thy table: tut, a toy!
      An old Italian fox is not so kind, my boy.   *Exit.*

TRA: A vengeance on your crafty wither'd hide!
      Yet I have faced it with a card of ten.
      'Tis in my head to do my master good:
415   I see no reason but supposed Lucentio
      Must get a father, call'd 'supposed Vincentio;'
      And that's a wonder: fathers commonly
      Do get their children; but in this case of wooing,
      A child shall get a sire, if I fail not of my cunning.

                                   Exit.

ACT III

SCENE I
[Padua. Baptista's house.]

Enter Lucentio, [as Cambio] Hortensio, [as Licio] and Bianca.

Luc: Fiddler, forbear;[1] you grow too forward, sir:
    Have you so soon forgot the entertainment
    Her sister Katharina welcomed you withal?
Hor: But, wrangling pedant,[2] this is
5   The patroness[3] of heavenly harmony:
    Then give me leave to have prerogative;
    And when in music we have spent an hour,
    Your lecture shall have leisure for as much.
Luc: Preposterous ass, that never read so far
10   To know the cause why music was ordain'd!
    Was it not to refresh the mind of man
    After his studies or his usual pain?
    Then give me leave to read philosophy,
    And while I pause, serve in your harmony.
15 Hor: Sirrah, I will not bear these braves[4] of thine.
Bia: Why, gentlemen, you do me double wrong,
    To strive for that which resteth in my choice:
    I am no breeching[5] scholar[†] in the schools;
    I'll not be tied to hours nor 'pointed times,
20   But learn my lessons as I please myself.
    And, to cut off all strife, here sit we down:
    Take you your instrument, play you the whiles;
    His lecture will be done ere you have tuned.
Hor: You'll leave his lecture when I am in tune?
25 Luc: That will be never: tune your instrument.
Bia: Where left we last?
Luc: Here, madam:

[1] *hold off*

[2] *small-minded teacher*

[3] *Minerva*[†]

[4] *insults*

[5] *(as in wearing breeches)*

'Hic ibat Simois; hic est Sigeia tellus;
Hic steterat Priami regia celsa senis.'[6]

30 BIA: Construe them.

LUC: 'Hic ibat,' as I told you before,–'Simois,' I am
Lucentio,–'hic est,' son unto Vincentio of Pisa,–
'Sigeia tellus,' disguised thus to get your love;–
'Hic steterat,' and that Lucentio that comes

35   a-wooing,–'Priami,' is my man Tranio,–'regia,'
bearing my port,–'celsa senis,' that we might
beguile the old pantaloon.[7]

HOR: Madam, my instrument's in tune.

BIA: Let's hear. O fie! the treble[8] jars.

40 LUC: Spit in the hole, man, and tune again.

BIA: Now let me see if I can construe it: 'Hic ibat
Simois,' I know you not,–'hic est Sigeia tellus,'
I trust you not,–'Hic steterat Priami,' take heed
he hear us not,–'regia,' presume not,–'celsa

45   senis,' despair not.

HOR: Madam, 'tis now in tune.

LUC: All but the bass.[9]

HOR: The base is right; 'tis the base knave that jars.
How fiery and forward our pedant is!

50   Now, for my life, the knave doth court my love:
Pedascule, I'll watch you better yet.

BIA: In time I may believe, yet I mistrust.

LUC: Mistrust it not: for, sure, Æacides[10]
Was Ajax, call'd so from his grandfather.

55 BIA: I must believe my master; else, I promise you,
I should be arguing still upon that doubt:
But let it rest. Now, Licio, to you:
Good masters, take it not unkindly, pray,
That I have been thus pleasant with you both.

60 HOR: You may go walk, and give me leave a while:
My lessons make no music in three parts.

LUC: Are you so formal, sir? well, I must wait,
And watch withal; for, but I be deceived,
Our fine musician groweth amorous.

65 HOR: Madam, before you touch the instrument,
To learn the order of my fingering,
I must begin with rudiments of art;

[6] *"Here passed the Simois, here is the Sigeian earth; here stood the high kingdom of elderly Priam"*[†]

[7] *fool*[†]

[8] *treble string*

[9] *bass string; Hortensio puns on "base," meaning "lowly, no-good."*

[10] *another character from Ovid*[†]

To teach you gamut[11] in a briefer sort,
More pleasant, pithy and effectual,
70   Than hath been taught by any of my trade:
And there it is in writing, fairly drawn.

BIA: Why, I am past my gamut long ago.

HOR: Yet read the gamut† of Hortensio.

BIA: 'Gamut' I am, the ground of all accord,
75   'A re,' to plead Hortensio's passion;
'B mi,' Bianca, take him for thy lord,
'C fa ut,' that loves with all affection:
'D sol re,' one clef, two notes have I:
'E la mi,' show pity, or I die.'
80   Call you this gamut? tut, I like it not:
Old fashions please me best; I am not so nice,[12]
To change true rules for odd inventions.

Enter a Messenger [Nicke.]

NIC: Mistress, your father prays you leave your books
And help to dress your sister's chamber up:
85   You know to-morrow is the wedding-day.

BIA: Farewell, sweet masters both; I must be gone.

LUC: Faith, mistress, then I have no cause to stay.

HOR: But I have cause to pry into this pedant:
Methinks he looks as though he were in love:
90   Yet if thy thoughts, Bianca, be so humble
To cast thy wandering eyes on every stale,
Seize thee that list:[13] if once I find thee ranging,
Hortensio will be quit with thee by changing.   *Exit.*

[11]*scales in which notes are represented by sounds; Do, Re, Mi*

[12]*silly*

[13]*like*

SCENE II
[Padua. Before Baptista's house.]

*Enter Baptista, Gremio, Tranio, Katharina, Bianca,
[Lucentio,] and others, attendants.*

BAP: Signior Lucentio, this is the 'pointed day
  That Katharina and Petruchio should be married,
  And yet we hear not of our son-in-law.
  What will be said? what mockery will it be,
5 To want the bridegroom when the priest attends
  To speak the ceremonial rites of marriage!
  What says Lucentio to this shame of ours?
KAT: No shame but mine: I must, forsooth,[14] be forced
  To give my hand opposed against my heart
10 Unto a mad-brain rudesby[15] full of spleen;
  Who woo'd in haste and means to wed at leisure.
  I told you, I, he was a frantic fool,
  Hiding his bitter jests in blunt behavior:
  And, to be noted for a merry man,
15 He'll woo a thousand, 'point the day of marriage,
  Make feasts, invite friends, and proclaim the banns;
  Yet never means to wed where he hath woo'd.
  Now must the world point at poor Katharina,
  And say, 'Lo, there is mad Petruchio's wife,
20 If it would please him come and marry her!'
TRA: Patience, good Katharina, and Baptista too.
  Upon my life, Petruchio means but well,
  Whatever fortune stays him from his word:
  Though he be blunt, I know him passing wise;
25 Though he be merry, yet withal he's honest.
KAT: Would Katharina had never seen him though!
               Exit weeping.
BAP: Go, girl; I cannot blame thee now to weep;
  For such an injury would vex a very saint,
  Much more a shrew of thy impatient humour.[16]

Enter Biondello.

30 BIO: Master, master! news, old news, and such news as you
  never heard of!

---

[14]*in truth*

[15]*savage*

[16]*character*

Bap: Is it new and old too? how may that be?

Bio: Why, is it not news, to hear of Petruchio's coming?

Bap: Is he come?

35 Bio: Why, no, sir.

Bap: What then?

Bio: He is coming.

Bap: When will he be here?

Bio: When he stands where I am and sees you there.

40 Tra: But say, what to thine old news?

Bio: Why, Petruchio is coming in a new hat and an old jer-
kin,[17] a pair of old breeches thrice turned, a pair of boots
that have been candle-cases, one buckled, another laced,
an old rusty sword ta'en out of the town-armory, with a

45 broken hilt, and chapeless;[18] with two broken points: his
horse hipped[19] with an old mothy saddle and stirrups of
no kindred; besides, possessed with the glanders[20] and like
to mose in the chine;[†] troubled with the lampass, infected
with the fashions, full of wind-galls, sped with spavins,

50 rayed with yellows, past cure of the fives, stark spoiled
with the staggers, begnawn with the bots, swayed in the
back and shoulder-shotten;[21] near-legged[22] before and with
a half-chequed[23] bit and a head-stall[24] of sheep's leather
which, being restrained to keep him from stumbling, hath

55 been often burst and now repaired with knots; one girth[25]
six time pieced and a woman's crupper[26] of velure,[27] which
hath two letters for her name fairly set down in studs, and
here and there pieced with packthread.

Bap: Who comes with him?

60 Bio: O, sir, his lackey, for all the world caparisoned[28] like the
horse; with a linen stock on one leg and a kersey[29] boot-
hose on the other, gartered with a red and blue list;[30] an
old hat and 'the humour of forty fancies'[31] pricked[32] in't
for a feather: a monster, a very monster in apparel, and

65 not like a Christian footboy or a gentleman's lackey.

Tra: 'Tis some odd humour pricks him to this fashion;
Yet oftentimes he goes but mean-apparell'd.

Bap: I am glad he's come, howsoe'er he comes.

Bio: Why, sir, he comes not.

70 Bap: Didst thou not say he comes?

Bio: Who? that Petruchio came?

---

[17]*close-fitting jacket*

[18]*having no cover*

[19]*lameness in the hip*

[20]*horse disease [lines 48-51 describe other such diseases†]*

[21]*with a sprained or dislocated shoulder*

[22]*knock-kneed*

[23]*loose bridle in a horse's mouth*

[24]*bridle head-piece*

[25]*saddle-belt (fastened around a horse's stomach)*

[26]*saddle-strap (looped under a horse's tail)*

[27]*velvet*

[28]*outfitted*

[29]*coarse cloth*

[30]*strip of cloth*

[31]*whimsical ornamentation†*

[32]*pinned*

BAP: Ay, that Petruchio came.

BIO: No, sir, I say his horse comes, with him on his back.

BAP: Why, that's all one.

75 BIO: Nay, by Saint Jamy,
       I hold you a penny,
       A horse and a man
       Is more than one,
       And yet not many.

Enter Petruchio and Grumio.

80 PET: Come, where be these gallants? who's at home?

BAP: You are welcome, sir.

PET: And yet I come not well.

BAP: And yet you halt not.

TRA: Not so well apparell'd

85   As I wish you were.

PET: Were it better, I should rush in thus.
       But where is Kate? where is my lovely bride?
       How does my father? Gentles, methinks you frown:
       And wherefore gaze this goodly company,

90   As if they saw some wondrous monument,
       Some comet or unusual prodigy?[33]

BAP: Why, sir, you know this is your wedding-day:
       First were we sad, fearing you would not come;
       Now sadder, that you come so unprovided.[34]

95   Fie, doff this habit, shame to your estate,
       An eye-sore to our solemn festival!

TRA: And tell us, what occasion of import
       Hath all so long detain'd you from your wife,
       And sent you hither so unlike yourself?

100 PET: Tedious it were to tell, and harsh to hear:
       Sufficeth, I am come to keep my word,
       Though in some part enforced to digress;
       Which, at more leisure, I will so excuse
       As you shall well be satisfied withal.

105   But where is Kate? I stay too long from her:
       The morning wears, 'tis time we were at church.

TRA: See not your bride in these unreverent robes:
       Go to my chamber; put on clothes of mine.

[33]*supernatural sign*

[34]*unprepared*

PET: Not I, believe me: thus I'll visit her.
110 BAP: But thus, I trust, you will not marry her.
PET: Good sooth, even thus; therefore ha' done with words:
To me she's married, not unto my clothes:
Could I repair what she will wear in me,
As I can change these poor accoutrements,[35]   [35]*clothes*
115 'Twere well for Kate and better for myself.
But what a fool am I to chat with you,
When I should bid good morrow to my bride,
And seal the title with a lovely kiss!

                                                      Exit.

TRA: He hath some meaning in his mad attire:
120 We will persuade him, be it possible,
To put on better ere he go to church.
BAP: I'll after him, and see the event of this.

                                                      Exit.

TRA: But to her love concerneth us to add
Her father's liking: which to bring to pass,
125 As I before imparted to your worship,
I am to get a man,—whate'er he be,
It skills not much, we'll fit him to our turn,—
And he shall be Vincentio of Pisa;
And make assurance here in Padua
130 Of greater sums than I have promised.
So shall you quietly enjoy your hope,
And marry sweet Bianca with consent.
LUC: Were it not that my fellow-schoolmaster
Doth watch Bianca's steps so narrowly,
135 'twere good, methinks, to steal our marriage;
Which once perform'd, let all the world say no,
I'll keep mine own, despite of all the world.
TRA: That by degrees we mean to look into,
And watch our vantage in this business:
140 We'll over-reach the greybeard, Gremio,
The narrow-prying father, Minola,
The quaint musician, amorous Licio;
All for my master's sake, Lucentio.

Enter Gremio.
Signior Gremio, came you from the church?

145 GRE: As willingly as e'er I came from school.

    TRA: And is the bride and bridegroom coming home?

    GRE: A bridegroom say you? 'Tis a groom indeed,

      A grumbling groom, and that the girl shall find.

    TRA: Curster than she? why, 'tis impossible.

150 GRE: Why he's a devil, a devil, a very fiend.

    TRA: Why, she's a devil, a devil, the devil's dam.

    GRE: Tut, she's a lamb, a dove, a fool to him!

      I'll tell you, Sir Lucentio: when the priest

      Should ask, if Katharina should be his wife,

155   'Ay, by gogs-wouns,'[36] quoth he; and swore so loud,

      That, all-amazed, the priest let fall the book;

      And, as he stoop'd again to take it up,

      The mad-brain'd bridegroom took him such a cuff

      That down fell priest and book, and book and priest:

160   'Now take them up,' quoth he, 'if any list.'

    TRA: What said the wench when he rose again?

    GRE: Trembled and shook; for why, he stamp'd and swore,

      As if the vicar meant to cozen[37] him.

      But after many ceremonies done,

165   He calls for wine: 'A health!'[38] quoth he, as if

      He had been aboard, carousing to his mates

      After a storm; quaff'd off the muscadel[39]

      And threw the sops[40] all in the sexton's face;

      Having no other reason

170   But that his beard grew thin and hungerly

      And seem'd to ask him sops as he was drinking.

      This done, he took the bride about the neck

      And kiss'd her lips with such a clamorous smack

      That at the parting all the church did echo:

175   And I seeing this came thence for very shame;

      And after me, I know, the rout[41] is coming.

      Such a mad marriage never was before:

      Hark, hark! I hear the minstrels play. *Music plays.*

Enter Petruchio, Kate, Bianca, Baptista, Hortensio, [Grumio.]

PET: Gentlemen and friends, I thank you for your pains:

180   I know you think to dine with me to-day,

---

[36]*"by God's wounds" (an oath)*

[37]*cheat*

[38]*"a toast!"*

[39]*sweet wine*

[40]*pieces of cake soaked in wine*

[41]*crowd*

And have prepared great store of wedding cheer;
But so it is, my haste doth call me hence,
And therefore here I mean to take my leave.

BAP: Is't possible you will away to-night?

185 PET: I must away to-day, before night come:
Make it no wonder; if you knew my business,
You would entreat me rather go than stay.
And, honest company, I thank you all,
That have beheld me give away myself

190   To this most patient, sweet and virtuous wife:
Dine with my father, drink a health to me;
For I must hence; and farewell to you all.

TRA: Let us entreat you stay till after dinner.

PET: It may not be.

195 GRE: Let me entreat you.

PET: It cannot be.

KAT: Let me entreat you.

PET: I am content.

KAT: Are you content to stay?

200 PET: I am content you shall entreat me stay;
But yet not stay, entreat me how you can.

KAT: Now, if you love me, stay.

PET: Grumio, my horse.

GRU: Ay, sir, they be ready: the oats have eaten the horses.

205 KAT: Nay, then,
Do what thou canst, I will not go to-day;
No, nor to-morrow, not till I please myself.
The door is open, sir; there lies your way;
You may be jogging whiles your boots are green;[42]

210   For me, I'll not be gone till I please myself:
'Tis like you'll prove a jolly surly groom,
That take it on you at the first so roundly.[43]

PET: O Kate, content thee; prithee, be not angry.

KAT: I will be angry: what hast thou to do?

215   Father, be quiet; he shall stay my leisure.

GRE: Ay, marry, sir, now it begins to work.

KAT: Gentlemen, forward to the bridal dinner:
I see a woman may be made a fool,
If she had not a spirit to resist.

220 PET: They shall go forward, Kate, at thy command.

[42]*an idiom meaning "make the most of the time you have."*

[43]*bluntly*

Obey the bride, you that attend on her;
Go to the feast, revel and domineer,
Carouse full measure to her maidenhead,
Be mad and merry, or go hang yourselves:
225   But for my bonny Kate, she must with me.
Nay, look not big, nor stamp, nor stare, nor fret;
I will be master of what is mine own:
She is my goods, my chattels;[44] she is my house,
My household stuff, my field, my barn,
230   My horse, my ox, my ass, my any thing;
And here she stands, touch her whoever dare;
I'll bring mine action on the proudest he
That stops my way in Padua. Grumio,
Draw forth thy weapon, we are beset with thieves;
235   Rescue thy mistress, if thou be a man.
Fear not, sweet wench, they shall not touch thee, Kate:
I'll buckler thee against a million.

            [Exeunt Petruchio, Katharina, and Grumio.]

BAP: Nay, let them go, a couple of quiet ones.
GRE: Went they not quickly, I should die with laughing.
240 TRA: Of all mad matches never was the like.
LUC: Mistress, what's your opinion of your sister?
BIA: That, being mad herself, she's madly mated.
GRE: I warrant him, Petruchio is Kated.
BAP: Neighbours and friends, though bride and
245   bridegroom wants
For to supply the places at the table,
You know there wants no junkets[45] at the feast.
Lucentio, you shall supply the bridegroom's place:
And let Bianca take her sister's room.
250 TRA: Shall sweet Bianca practise how to bride it?
BAP: She shall, Lucentio. Come, gentlemen, let's go.

                                Exeunt.

---

[44]*movable property (The term is often applied to slaves.)*

[45]*appetizers*

ACT IV

[SCENE I]
[Petruchio's country house.]

Enter Grumio.

GRU: Fie, fie on all tired jades, on all mad masters, and all foul
ways! Was ever man so beaten? was ever man so rayed?
was ever man so weary? I am sent before to make a fire,
and they are coming after to warm them. Now, were not
5   I a little pot and soon hot, my very lips might freeze to
my teeth, my tongue to the roof of my mouth, my heart
in my belly, ere I should come by a fire to thaw me: but I,
with blowing the fire, shall warm myself; for, considering
the weather, a taller man than I will take cold. Holla, ho!
10   Curtis!

Enter Curtis.

CUR: Who is that calls so coldly?
GRU: A piece of ice: if thou doubt it, thou mayst slide from
my shoulder to my heel with no greater a run but my
head and my neck. A fire, good Curtis.
15 CUR: Is my master and his wife coming, Grumio?
GRU: O, ay, Curtis, ay: and therefore fire, fire; cast on no
water.
CUR: Is she so hot a shrew as she's reported?
GRU: She was, good Curtis, before this frost: but, thou know-
20   est, winter tames man, woman, and beast; for it hath
tamed my old master and my new mistress and myself,
fellow Curtis.
CUR: Away, you three-inch fool! I am no beast.
GRU: Am I but three inches? why, thy horn† is a foot; and so

25   long am I at the least. But wilt thou make a fire, or shall I
      complain on thee to our mistress, whose hand, she being
      now at hand, thou shalt soon feel, to thy cold comfort,
      for being slow in thy hot office?

CUR: I prithee, good Grumio, tell me, how goes the world?

30 GRU: A cold world, Curtis, in every office but thine; and
      therefore fire: do thy duty, and have thy duty; for my
      master and mistress are almost frozen to death.

CUR: There's fire ready; and therefore, good Grumio, the
      news.

35 GRU: Why, 'Jack, boy!† ho! boy!' and as much news as will
      thaw.

CUR: Come, you are so full of cony¹-catching!

GRU: Why, therefore fire; for I have caught extreme cold.
      Where's the cook? is supper ready, the house trimmed,
40   rushes strewed, cobwebs swept; the serving-men in their
      new fustian,² their white stockings, and every officer his
      wedding-garment on? Be the Jacks³ fair within, the Jills⁴
      fair without, the carpets laid, and every thing in order?

CUR: All ready; and therefore, I pray thee, news.

45 GRU: First, know, my horse is tired; my master and mis-
      tress fallen out.

CUR: How?

GRU: Out of their saddles into the dirt; and thereby hangs a
      tale.

50 CUR: Let's ha't, good Grumio.

GRU: Lend thine ear.

CUR: Here.

GRU: There.

CUR: This is to feel a tale, not to hear a tale.

55 GRU: And therefore 'tis called a sensible tale: and this cuff
      was but to knock at your ear, and beseech listening. Now
      I begin: Inprimis,⁵ we came down a foul hill, my master
      riding behind my mistress,—

CUR: Both of one horse?

60 GRU: What's that to thee?

CUR: Why, a horse.

GRU: Tell thou the tale: but hadst thou not crossed me, thou
      shouldst have heard how her horse fell and she under
      her horse; thou shouldst have heard in how miry a place,
65   how she was bemoiled,⁶ how he left her with the horse

---

¹rabbit; also a sexual pun

²coarse cloth

³leather cups (also "boys")

⁴measuring cups (also "girls")

⁵in the first place

⁶dirtied

upon her, how he beat me because her horse stumbled,
how she waded through the dirt to pluck him off me,
how he swore, how she prayed, that never prayed before,
how I cried, how the horses ran away, how her bridle was
70   burst, how I lost my crupper, with many things of worthy
memory, which now shall die in oblivion and thou return
unexperienced to thy grave.

CUR: By this reckoning he is more shrew than she.

GRU: Ay; and that thou and the proudest of you all shall find
75   when he comes home. But what talk I of this? Call forth
Nathaniel, Joseph, Nicholas, Philip, Walter, Sugarsop
and the rest: let their heads be sleekly combed, their blue
coats brushed, and their garters of an indifferent[7] knit: let
them curtsy with their left legs and not presume to touch
80   a hair of my master's horse-tail till they kiss their hands.
Are they all ready?

CUR: They are.

GRU: Call them forth.

CUR: Do you hear, ho? you must meet my master to counte-
85   nance my mistress.

GRU: Why, she hath a face of her own.

CUR: Who knows not that?

GRU: Thou, it seems, that calls for company to countenance
her.

90 CUR: I call them forth to credit her.

Enter four or five serving men.

GRU: Why, she comes to borrow nothing of them.

NAT: Welcome home, Grumio!

PHI: How now, Grumio!

JOS: What, Grumio!

95 NIC: Fellow Grumio!

NAT: How now, old lad?

GRU: Welcome, you;—how now, you;—what, you;—fellow,
you;—and thus much for greeting. Now, my spruce[8]
companions, is all ready, and all things neat?

100 NAT: All things is ready. How near is our master?

GRU: E'en at hand, alighted by this; and therefore be not—
Cock's passion,[9] silence! I hear my master.

[7]*ordinary pattern or texture*

[8]*lively*

[9]*by Christ's suffer-ing (an oath)*

Enter Petruchio and Katharina.

PET: Where be these knaves? What, no man at door
    To hold my stirrup nor to take my horse!
105   Where is Nathaniel, Gregory, Philip?
ALL SERVING-MEN: Here, here, sir; here, sir.
PET: Here, sir! here, sir! here, sir! here, sir!
    You logger-headed and unpolish'd grooms!
    What, no attendance? no regard? no duty?
110   Where is the foolish knave I sent before?
GRU: Here, sir; as foolish as I was before.
PET: You peasant swain! you whoreson malt-horse drudge!
    Did I not bid thee meet me in the park,
    And bring along these rascal knaves with thee?
115 GRU: Nathaniel's coat, sir, was not fully made,
    And Gabriel's pumps were all unpink'd[10] i' the heel;
    There was no link[11] to colour Peter's hat,
    And Walter's dagger was not come from sheathing:
    There were none fine but Adam, Ralph, and Gregory;
120   The rest were ragged, old, and beggarly;
    Yet, as they are, here are they come to meet you.
PET: Go, rascals, go, and fetch my supper in.
                       Exeunt Servants.

    Where is the life that late I led—
    Where are those—Sit down, Kate, and welcome.—
    Soud,[12] soud, soud, soud!

Enter servants with supper.
125   Why, when, I say? Nay, good sweet Kate, be merry.
    Off with my boots, you rogues! you villains, when?
        It was the friar of orders grey,
          As he forth walked on his way:—
    Out, you rogue! you pluck my foot[†] awry:
130   Take that, and mend the plucking off the other.
    Be merry, Kate. Some water, here; what, ho!
Enter one with water.
    Where's my spaniel Troilus? Sirrah, get you hence,
    And bid my cousin Ferdinand come hither:
    One, Kate, that you must kiss, and be acquainted with.
135   Where are my slippers? Shall I have some water?

[10]*undecorated*

[11]*torch, the smoke of which could be used to blacken old hats.*

[12]*an expression of impatience*

Come, Kate, and wash, and welcome heartily.
You whoreson villain! will you let it fall?
KAT: Patience, I pray you; 'twas a fault unwilling.
PET: A whoreson beetle-headed, flap-ear'd knave!
140   Come, Kate, sit down; I know you have a stomach.
Will you give thanks, sweet Kate; or else shall I?
What's this? mutton?
SER: Ay.
PET: Who brought it?
145 PETER: I.
PET: 'Tis burnt; and so is all the meat.
What dogs are these! Where is the rascal cook?
How durst you, villains, bring it from the dresser,
And serve it thus to me that love it not?
150   There, take it to you, trenchers, cups, and all;
You heedless joltheads and unmanner'd slaves!
What, do you grumble? I'll be with you straight.
KAT: I pray you, husband, be not so disquiet:
The meat was well, if you were so contented.
155 PET: I tell thee, Kate, 'twas burnt and dried away;
And I expressly am forbid to touch it,
For it engenders choler,[13] planteth anger;
And better 'twere that both of us did fast,
Since, of ourselves, ourselves are choleric,
160   Than feed it with such over-roasted flesh.
Be patient; to-morrow 't shall be mended,
And, for this night, we'll fast for company:
Come, I will bring thee to thy bridal chamber.

                                      Exeunt.

Enter Servants severally.

NAT: Peter, didst ever see the like?
165 PETER: He kills her in her own humour.

Enter Curtis a servant.

GRU: Where is he?
CUR: In her chamber, making a sermon of continency to her;
And rails, and swears, and rates, that she, poor soul,

[13]*bile, thought to cause irritability and anger*†

Knows not which way to stand, to look, to speak,
170   And sits as one new-risen from a dream.
Away, away! for he is coming hither.   *Exeunt.*

Enter Petruchio.

PET: Thus have I politicly[14] begun my reign,
And 'tis my hope to end successfully.
My falcon[15] now is sharp and passing empty;[†]
175   And till she stoop she must not be full-gorged,
For then she never looks upon her lure.
Another way I have to man my haggard,[16]
To make her come and know her keeper's call,
That is, to watch her, as we watch these kites[17]
180   That bate[18] and beat and will not be obedient.
She eat no meat to-day, nor none shall eat;
Last night she slept not, nor to-night she shall not;
As with the meat, some undeserved fault
I'll find about the making of the bed;
185   And here I'll fling the pillow, there the bolster,
This way the coverlet, another way the sheets:
Ay, and amid this hurly I intend
That all is done in reverend[19] care of her;
And in conclusion she shall watch all night:
190   And if she chance to nod I'll rail and brawl
And with the clamour keep her still awake.
This is a way to kill a wife with kindness;
And thus I'll curb her mad and headstrong humour.
He that knows better how to tame a shrew,
195   Now let him speak: 'tis charity to show.   *Exit.*

[SCENE II]
[Padua. Before Baptista's house.]

Enter Tranio and Hortensio.

TRA: Is't possible, friend Licio, that Mistress Bianca
Doth fancy any other but Lucentio?
I tell you, sir, she bears me fair in hand.

[14]*shrewdly*

[15]*Petruchio compares Kate to a trained falcon in lines 177-183.*

[16]*wild female hawk*

[17]*scavenging birds*

[18]*flutter*

[19]*respectful*

HOR: Sir, to satisfy you in what I have said,
5   Stand by and mark the manner of his teaching.

Enter Bianca and Lucentio.

LUC: Now, mistress, profit you in what you read?
BIA: What, master, read you? first resolve me that.
LUC: I read that I profess, the Art to Love.[20]
BIA: And may you prove, sir, master of your art!
10 LUC: While you, sweet dear, prove mistress of my heart!
HOR: Quick proceeders, marry![21] Now, tell me, I pray,
        You that durst swear that your mistress Bianca
        Loved none in the world so well as Lucentio.
TRA: O despiteful love! unconstant womankind!
15   I tell thee, Licio, this is wonderful.[22]
HOR: Mistake no more: I am not Licio,
        Nor a musician, as I seem to be;
        But one that scorn to live in this disguise,
        For such a one as leaves a gentleman,
20   And makes a god of such a cullion:[23]
        Know, sir, that I am call'd Hortensio.
TRA: Signior Hortensio, I have often heard
        Of your entire affection to Bianca;
        And since mine eyes are witness of her lightness,[24]
25   I will with you, if you be so contented,
        Forswear Bianca and her love for ever.
HOR: See, how they kiss and court! Signior Lucentio,
        Here is my hand, and here I firmly vow
        Never to woo her no more, but do forswear her,
30   As one unworthy all the former favours
        That I have fondly flatter'd her withal.
TRA: And here I take the unfeigned oath,
        Never to marry with her though she would entreat:
        Fie on her! see, how beastly she doth court him!
35 HOR: Would all the world but he had quite forsworn![25]
        For me, that I may surely keep mine oath,
        I will be married to a wealthy widow,
        Ere three days pass, which hath as long loved me
        As I have loved this proud disdainful haggard.
40   And so farewell, Signior Lucentio.
        Kindness in women, not their beauteous looks,

[20]*Ovid's Ars Amatoria†*

[21]*by the Virgin Mary (an oath)*

[22]*amazing*

[23]*scoundrel*

[24]*lack of loyalty*

[25]*proved untrue*

      Shall win my love: and so I take my leave,

      In resolution as I swore before.   *[Exit.]*

Tra: Mistress Bianca, bless you with such grace

45   As 'longeth to a lover's blessed case!

      Nay, I have ta'en you napping, gentle love,

      And have forsworn you with Hortensio.

Bia: Tranio, you jest: but have you both forsworn me?

50 Tra: Mistress, we have.

Luc: Then we are rid of Licio.

Tra: I' faith, he'll have a lusty widow now,

      That shall be woo'd and wedded in a day.

Bia: God give him joy!

55 Tra: Ay, and he'll tame her.

Bia: He says so, Tranio.

Tra: Faith, he is gone unto the taming-school.

Bia: The taming-school! what, is there such a place?

Tra: Ay, mistress, and Petruchio is the master;

60   That teacheth tricks eleven and twenty long,

      To tame a shrew and charm her chattering tongue.

Enter Biondello.

Bio: O master, master, I have watch'd so long

      That I am dog-weary: but at last I spied

      An ancient angel coming down the hill,

65   Will serve the turn.

Tra: What is he, Biondello?

Bio: Master, a mercatante,[26] or a pedant,

      I know not what; but formal in apparel,

      In gait and countenance surely like a father.

70 Luc: And what of him, Tranio?

Tra: If he be credulous and trust my tale,

      I'll make him glad to seem Vincentio,

      And give assurance to Baptista Minola,

      As if he were the right Vincentio.

75   Take in your love, and then let me alone.

                  [Exeunt Lucentio and Bianca.]

Enter a Pedant.

[26]*merchant*

PED: God save you, sir!

TRA: And you, sir! you are welcome.
     Travel you far on, or are you at the farthest?

PED: Sir, at the farthest for a week or two:
80   But then up farther, and as far as Rome;
     And so to Tripoli,† if God lend me life.

TRA: What countryman, I pray?

PED: Of Mantua.

TRA: Of Mantua, sir? marry, God forbid!
85   And come to Padua, careless of your life?

PED: My life, sir! how, I pray? for that goes hard.

TRA: 'Tis death for any one in Mantua
     To come to Padua. Know you not the cause?
     Your ships are stay'd at Venice, and the duke,
90   For private quarrel 'twixt your duke and him,
     Hath publish'd and proclaim'd it openly:
     'Tis marvel, but that you are but newly come,
     You might have heard it else proclaim'd about.

PED: Alas! sir, it is worse for me than so;
95   For I have bills for money by exchange
     From Florence and must here deliver them.

TRA: Well, sir, to do you courtesy,
     This will I do, and this I will advise you:
     First, tell me, have you ever been at Pisa?

100 PED: Ay, sir, in Pisa have I often been,
     Pisa renowned for grave citizens.

TRA: Among them know you one Vincentio?

PED: I know him not, but I have heard of him;
     A merchant of incomparable wealth.

105 TRA: He is my father, sir; and, sooth to say,
     In countenance somewhat doth resemble you.

BIO: As much as an apple doth an oyster, and all one.

TRA: To save your life in this extremity,[27]
     This favour will I do you for his sake;
110   And think it not the worst of all your fortunes
     That you are like to Sir Vincentio.
     His name and credit shall you undertake,
     And in my house you shall be friendly lodged:
     Look that you take upon you as you should;
115   You understand me, sir: so shall you stay

[27] *urgent moment*

Till you have done your business in the city:
If this be courtesy, sir, accept of it.
PED: O sir, I do; and will repute you ever
The patron of my life and liberty.
120 TRA: Then go with me to make the matter good.
This, by the way, I let you understand;
my father is here look'd for every day,
To pass assurance of a dower in marriage
'Twixt me and one Baptista's daughter here:
125   In all these circumstances I'll instruct you:
Go with me to clothe you as becomes you.

Exeunt.

[SCENE III]
[A room in Petruchio's house.]

Enter Katharina and Grumio.

GRU: No, no, forsooth; I dare not for my life.
KAT: The more my wrong, the more his spite appears:
What, did he marry me to famish me?
Beggars, that come unto my father's door,
5   Upon entreaty have a present alms;
If not, elsewhere they meet with charity:
But I, who never knew how to entreat,
Nor never needed that I should entreat,
Am starved for meat, giddy for lack of sleep,
10   With oath kept waking and with brawling fed:
And that which spites me more than all these wants,
He does it under name of perfect love;
As who should say, if I should sleep or eat,
'Twere deadly sickness or else present death.
15   I prithee go and get me some repast;
I care not what, so it be wholesome food.
GRU: What say you to a neat's[28] foot?
KAT: 'Tis passing good: I prithee let me have it.
GRU: I fear it is too choleric a meat.
20   How say you to a fat tripe[29] finely broil'd?

[28]*calf's*

[29]*cow's stomach*

KAT: I like it well: good Grumio, fetch it me.

GRU: I cannot tell; I fear 'tis choleric.
      What say you to a piece of beef and mustard?

KAT: A dish that I do love to feed upon.

25 GRU: Ay, but the mustard is too hot a little.

KAT: Why then, the beef, and let the mustard rest.

GRU: Nay then, I will not: you shall have the mustard,
      Or else you get no beef of Grumio.

KAT: Then both, or one, or any thing thou wilt.

30 GRU: Why then, the mustard without the beef.

KAT: Go, get thee gone, thou false deluding slave,

                                    Beats him.

      That feed'st me with the very name of meat:
      Sorrow on thee and all the pack of you,
      That triumph thus upon my misery!

35   Go, get thee gone, I say.

Enter Petruchio, and Hortensio with meat.

PET: How fares my Kate? What, sweeting, all amort?

HOR: Mistress, what cheer?

KAT: Faith, as cold as can be.

PET: Pluck up thy spirits; look cheerfully upon me.

40   Here love; thou see'st how diligent I am
      To dress thy meat myself and bring it thee:
      I am sure, sweet Kate, this kindness merits thanks.
      What, not a word? Nay, then thou lovest it not;
      And all my pains is sorted to no proof.

45   Here, take away this dish.

KAT: I pray you, let it stand.

PET: The poorest service is repaid with thanks;
      And so shall mine, before you touch the meat.

KAT: I thank you, sir.

50 HOR: Signior Petruchio, fie! you are to blame.
      Come, mistress Kate, I'll bear you company.

PET: Eat it up all, Hortensio, if thou lovest me.
      Much good do it unto thy gentle heart!
      Kate, eat apace: and now, my honey love,

55   Will we return unto thy father's house
      And revel it as bravely as the best,

With silken coats and caps and golden rings,

[30]petticoats

With ruffs and cuffs and farthingales[30] and things;

With scarfs and fans and double change of bravery,

60   With amber bracelets, beads and all this knavery.

What, hast thou dined? The tailor stays thy leisure,

To deck thy body with his ruffling treasure.

Enter Tailor.

Come, tailor, let us see these ornaments;

Lay forth the gown.

Enter Haberdasher.

65   What news with you, sir?

HAB: Here is the cap your worship did bespeak.

[31]soup bowl

PET: Why, this was moulded on a porringer;[31]

A velvet dish: fie, fie! 'tis lewd and filthy:

[32]seashell

Why, 'tis a cockle[32] or a walnut-shell,

70   A knack, a toy, a trick, a baby's cap:

Away with it! come, let me have a bigger.

KAT: I'll have no bigger: this doth fit the time,

And gentlewomen wear such caps as these.

PET: When you are gentle, you shall have one too,

75   And not till then.

HOR: That will not be in haste.

KAT: Why, sir, I trust I may have leave to speak;

And speak I will; I am no child, no babe:

Your betters have endured me say my mind,

80   And if you cannot, best you stop your ears.

My tongue will tell the anger of my heart,

Or else my heart concealing it will break,

And rather than it shall, I will be free

Even to the uttermost, as I please, in words.

85 PET: Why, thou say'st true; it is a paltry cap,

[33]crust

A custard-coffin,[33] a bauble, a silken pie:

I love thee well, in that thou likest it not.

KAT: Love me or love me not, I like the cap;

And it I will have, or I will have none.

[Exit Haberdasher.]

[34]like a costume for a masque (a short play)

90 PET: Thy gown? why, ay: come, tailor, let us see't.

O mercy, God! what masquing[34] stuff is here?

What's this? a sleeve? 'tis like a demi[35]-cannon:

What, up and down, carved like an apple-tart?

Here's snip and nip and cut and slish and slash,

95   Like to a censer[36] in a barber's shop:

Why, what, i' devil's name, tailor, call'st thou this?

HOR: I see she's like to have neither cap nor gown.

TAI: You bid me make it orderly and well,

According to the fashion and the time.

100 PET: Marry, and did; but if you be remember'd,

I did not bid you mar it to the time.

Go, hop me over every kennel home,[†]

For you shall hop without my custom,[37] sir:

I'll none of it: hence! make your best of it.

105 KAT: I never saw a better-fashion'd gown,

More quaint, more pleasing, nor more commendable:

Belike you mean to make a puppet of me.

PET: Why, true; he means to make a puppet of thee.

TAI: She says your worship means to make a puppet of her.

110 PET: O monstrous arrogance!

Thou liest, thou thread, thou thimble,[†]

Thou yard, three-quarters, half-yard, quarter, nail!

Thou flea, thou nit, thou winter-cricket thou!

Braved in mine own house with a skein of thread?

115   Away, thou rag, thou quantity, thou remnant;

Or I shall so be-mete[38] thee with thy yard[39]

As thou shalt think on prating whilst thou livest!

I tell thee, I, that thou hast marr'd her gown.

TAI: Your worship is deceived; the gown is made

120   Just as my master had direction:

Grumio gave order how it should be done.

GRU: I gave him no order; I gave him the stuff.

TAI: But how did you desire it should be made?

GRU: Marry, sir, with needle and thread.

125 TAI: But did you not request to have it cut?

GRU: Thou hast faced many things.

TAI: I have.

GRU: Face not me: thou hast braved many men; brave not

me; I will neither be faced nor braved. I say unto thee, I

130   bid thy master cut out the gown; but I did not bid him

cut it to pieces: ergo, thou liest.

---

[35]*half*

[36]*a fancy perfume vessel*

[37]*business*

[38]*measure out punishment upon; also "measure"*

[39]*measuring stick*

TAI: Why, here is the note of the fashion to testify.

PET: Read it.

GRU: The note lies in's throat, if he say I said so.

135 TAI: 'Imprimis, a loose-bodied gown:'

GRU: Master, if ever I said loose-bodied gown, sew me in
  the skirts of it, and beat me to death with a bottom of
  brown thread: I said a gown.

PET: Proceed.

140 TAI: 'With a small compassed cape:'

GRU: I confess the cape.

TAI: 'With a trunk sleeve:'

GRU: I confess two sleeves.

TAI: 'The sleeves curiously cut.'

145 PET: Ay, there's the villany.

GRU: Error i' the bill, sir; error i' the bill.
  I commanded the sleeves should be cut out and sewed
  up again; and that I'll prove upon thee, though thy little
  finger be armed in a thimble.

150 TAI: This is true that I say: an I had thee in place where,
  thou shouldst know it.

GRU: I am for thee straight: take thou the bill, give me thy
  mete-yard, and spare not me.

HOR: God-a-mercy, Grumio! then he shall have no odds.[40]

155 PET: Well, sir, in brief, the gown is not for me.

GRU: You are i' the right, sir: 'tis for my mistress.

PET: Go, take it up unto thy master's use.

GRU: Villain, not for thy life: take up my mistress' gown for
  thy master's use!

160 PET: Why, sir, what's your conceit[41] in that?

GRU: O, sir, the conceit is deeper than you think for:
  Take up my mistress' gown to his master's use!
  O, fie, fie, fie!

PET: Hortensio, say thou wilt see the tailor paid.

165   Go take it hence; be gone, and say no more.

HOR: Tailor, I'll pay thee for thy gown tomorrow:
  Take no unkindness of his hasty words:
  Away! I say; commend me to thy master.

            Exit Tailor.

PET: Well, come, my Kate; we will unto your father's

170   Even in these honest mean habiliments:[42]

[40]*chance of success*

[41]*idea*

[42]*clothes*

Our purses shall be proud, our garments poor;
For 'tis the mind that makes the body rich;
And as the sun breaks through the darkest clouds,
So honour peereth in the meanest habit.
175 What is the jay more precious than the lark,
Because his feathers are more beautiful?
Or is the adder[43] better than the eel,   [43]*snake*
Because his painted skin contents the eye?
O, no, good Kate; neither art thou the worse
180 For this poor furniture and mean array.
If thou account'st it shame, lay it on me;
And therefore frolic: we will hence forthwith,
To feast and sport us at thy father's house.
Go, call my men, and let us straight to him;
185 And bring our horses unto Long-lane end;
There will we mount, and thither walk on foot.
Let's see; I think 'tis now some seven o'clock,
And well we may come there by dinner-time.[44]   [44]*lunchtime*
KAT: I dare assure you, sir, 'tis almost two;
190 And 'twill be supper-time[45] ere you come there.   [45]*dinnertime*
PET: It shall be seven ere I go to horse:
Look, what I speak, or do, or think to do,
You are still crossing it. Sirs, let't alone:
I will not go to-day; and ere I do,
195 It shall be what o'clock I say it is.
HOR: Why, so this gallant will command the sun.

                                        [Exeunt.]

[SCENE IV]
[Padua. Before Baptista's house.]

Enter Tranio, and the Pedant dressed like Vincentio.

TRA: Sir, this is the house: please it you that I call?
PED: Ay, what else? and but I be deceived
Signior Baptista may remember me,
Near twenty years ago, in Genoa,
5 Where we were lodgers at the Pegasus.

TRA: 'Tis well; and hold your own, in any case,
       With such austerity⁴⁶ as 'longeth to a father.
PED: I warrant you.

Enter Biondello.
       But, sir, here comes your boy;
10   'Twere good he were school'd.⁴⁷
   TRA: Fear you not him. Sirrah Biondello,
       Now do your duty throughly, I advise you:
       Imagine 'twere the right Vincentio.
   BIO: Tut, fear not me.
15 TRA: But hast thou done thy errand to Baptista?
   BIO: I told him that your father was at Venice,
       And that you look'd for him this day in Padua.
   TRA: Thou'rt a tall⁴⁸ fellow: hold thee that to drink.
       Here comes Baptista: set your countenance, sir.

Enter Baptista and Lucentio: Pedant booted and bare headed.
20   Signior Baptista, you are happily met.
       Sir, this is the gentleman I told you of:
       I pray you stand good father to me now,
       Give me Bianca for my patrimony.
   PED: Soft, son!
25   Sir, by your leave: having come to Padua
       To gather in some debts, my son Lucentio
       Made me acquainted with a weighty cause
       Of love between your daughter and himself:
       And, for the good report I hear of you
30   And for the love he beareth to your daughter
       And she to him, to stay him not too long,
       I am content, in a good father's care,
       To have him match'd; and if you please to like
       No worse than I, upon some agreement
35   Me shall you find ready and willing
       With one consent to have her so bestow'd;
       For curious I cannot be with you,
       Signior Baptista, of whom I hear so well.
   BAP: Sir, pardon me in what I have to say:
40   Your plainness and your shortness please me well.
       Right true it is, your son Lucentio here

---

⁴⁶*plainness; serious-
ness*

⁴⁷*informed of the
plan*

⁴⁸*fine*

Doth love my daughter and she loveth him,
Or both dissemble deeply their affections:
And therefore, if you say no more than this,

45   That like a father you will deal with him
And pass my daughter a sufficient dower,
The match is made, and all is done:
Your son shall have my daughter with consent.

TRA: I thank you, sir. Where then do you know best

50   We be affied⁴⁹ and such assurance ta'en   ⁴⁹*engaged*
As shall with either part's agreement stand?

BAP: Not in my house, Lucentio; for, you know,
Pitchers have ears, and I have many servants:
Besides, old Gremio is hearkening⁵⁰ still;   ⁵⁰*eavesdropping*

55   And happily⁵¹ we might be interrupted.   ⁵¹*perhaps*

TRA: Then at my lodging, an it like you:
There doth my father lie; and there, this night,
We'll pass the business privately and well.
Send for your daughter by your servant here:

60   My boy shall fetch the scrivener⁵² presently.   ⁵²*notary*
The worst is this, that, at so slender warning,
You are like to have a thin and slender pittance.⁵³   ⁵³*meal*

BAP: It likes me well. Cambio, hie⁵⁴ you home,   ⁵⁴*hurry*
And bid Bianca make her ready straight;

65   And, if you will, tell what hath happened,
Lucentio's father is arrived in Padua,
And how she's like to be Lucentio's wife.

BIO: I pray the gods she may with all my heart!
                          Exit Biondello and Lucentio.

TRA: Dally not with the gods, but get thee gone.

70   Signior Baptista, shall I lead the way?
Welcome! one mess⁵⁵ is like to be your cheer: ⁵⁵*dish*
Come, sir; we will better it in Pisa.

BAP: I follow you.   *Exeunt.*

Enter Lucentio and Biondello.

BIO: Cambio!

75 LUC: What sayest thou, Biondello?
BIO: You saw my master wink and laugh upon you?
LUC: Biondello, what of that?
BIO: Faith, nothing; but has left me here behind, to expound⁵⁶   ⁵⁶*explain*

the meaning or moral of his signs and tokens.

80 Luc: I pray thee, moralize them.

Bio: Then thus. Baptista is safe, talking with the deceiving
father of a deceitful son.

Luc: And what of him?

Bio: His daughter is to be brought by you to the supper.

85 Luc: And then?

Bio: The old priest of Saint Luke's church is at your command at all hours.

Luc: And what of all this?

Bio: I cannot tell; except they are busied about a counterfeit
90   assurance: take you assurance[57] of her, 'cum privilegio ad imprimendum solum:'[58] to the church; take the
priest, clerk, and some sufficient honest witnesses:
If this be not that you look for, I have no more to say,
But bid Bianca farewell for ever and a day.

95 Luc: Hearest thou, Biondello?

Bio: I cannot tarry: I knew a wench married in an afternoon
as she went to the garden for parsley to stuff a rabbit;
and so may you, sir: and so, adieu, sir. My master hath
appointed me to go to Saint Luke's, to bid the priest be
100   ready to come against you come with your appendix.[59]

Exit.

Luc: I may, and will, if she be so contented:
She will be pleased; then wherefore should I doubt?
Hap what hap may, I'll roundly go about her:
It shall go hard if Cambio go without her.   *Exit.*

[SCENE V]
[A public road.]

Enter Petruchio, Kate, Hortensio.

Pet: Come on, i' God's name; once more toward our
father's.
Good Lord, how bright and goodly shines the moon!

Kat: The moon! the sun: it is not moonlight now.

5 Pet: I say it is the moon that shines so bright.

Kat: I know it is the sun that shines so bright.

Pet: Now, by my mother's son, and that's myself,

[57]*make yourself
sure*

[58]*"with the sole
right to print"*†

[59]*bride*

It shall be moon, or star, or what I list,
Or ere I journey to your father's house.
10   Go on, and fetch our horses back again.
Evermore cross'd and cross'd; nothing but cross'd!
HOR: Say as he says, or we shall never go.
KAT: Forward, I pray, since we have come so far,
And be it moon, or sun, or what you please:
15   An if you please to call it a rush-candle,
Henceforth I vow it shall be so for me.
PET: I say it is the moon.
KAT: I know it is the moon.
PET: Nay, then you lie: it is the blessed sun.
20 KAT: Then, God be bless'd, it is the blessed sun:
But sun it is not, when you say it is not;
And the moon changes even as your mind.
What you will have it named, even that it is;
And so it shall be so for Katharina.
25 HOR: Petruchio, go thy ways; the field is won.
PET: Well, forward, forward! thus the bowl should run,
And not unluckily against the bias.[60]
But, soft![61] company is coming here.

Enter Vincentio.

Good morrow, gentle mistress: where away?
30   Tell me, sweet Kate, and tell me truly too,
Hast thou beheld a fresher gentlewoman?
Such war of white and red within her cheeks!
What stars do spangle heaven with such beauty,
As those two eyes become that heavenly face?
35   Fair lovely maid, once more good day to thee.
Sweet Kate, embrace her for her beauty's sake.
HOR: A' will make the man mad, to make a woman of him.
KAT: Young budding virgin, fair and fresh and sweet,
Whither away, or where is thy abode?
40   Happy the parents of so fair a child;
Happier the man, whom favourable stars
Allot thee for his lovely bed-fellow!
PET: Why, how now, Kate! I hope thou art not mad:
This is a man, old, wrinkled, faded, wither'd,
45   And not a maiden, as thou say'st he is.

[60]*direction it should go*

[61]*quiet*

KAT: Pardon, old father, my mistaking eyes,
That have been so bedazzled with the sun
That everything I look on seemeth green:
Now I perceive thou art a reverend father;
50   Pardon, I pray thee, for my mad mistaking.
PET: Do, good old grandsire; and withal make known
Which way thou travellest: if along with us,
We shall be joyful of thy company.
VIN: Fair sir, and you my merry mistress,
55   That with your strange encounter much amazed me,
My name is call'd Vincentio; my dwelling Pisa;
And bound I am to Padua; there to visit
A son of mine, which long I have not seen.
PET: What is his name?
60 VIN: Lucentio, gentle sir.
PET: Happily met; the happier for thy son.
And now by law, as well as reverend age,
I may entitle thee my loving father:
The sister to my wife, this gentlewoman,
65   Thy son by this hath married. Wonder not,
Nor be grieved: she is of good esteem,
Her dowry wealthy, and of worthy birth;
Beside, so qualified as may beseem
The spouse of any noble gentleman.
70   Let me embrace with old Vincentio,
And wander we to see thy honest son,
Who will of thy arrival be full joyous.
VIN: But is it true? or else is it your pleasure,
Like pleasant travellers, to break a jest
75   Upon the company you overtake?
HOR: I do assure thee, father, so it is.
PET: Come, go along, and see the truth hereof;
For our first merriment hath made thee jealous.[62]

                    Exeunt [all but Hortensio.]

HOR: Well, Petruchio, this has put me in heart.
80   Have to my widow! and if she be froward,
Then hast thou taught Hortensio to be untoward.

                            Exit.

[62]*suspicious*

ACT V

[SCENE I]
[Padua. Before Lucentio's house.]

Enter Biondello, Lucentio and Bianca, Gremio is out before.

BIO: Softly and swiftly, sir; for the priest is ready.
LUC: I fly, Biondello: but they may chance to need thee at
    home; therefore leave us.   *Exit Lucentio and Bianca.*
BIO: Nay, faith, I'll see the church o'[1] your back; and then
5   come back to my master's as soon as I can.
                  [Exit Biondello.]
GRE: I marvel Cambio comes not all this while.

Enter Petruchio, Kate, Vincentio, Grumio with Attendants.

PET: Sir, here's the door, this is Lucentio's house:
    My father's bears more toward the market-place;
    Thither must I, and here I leave you, sir.
10 VIN: You shall not choose but drink before you go:
    I think I shall command your welcome here,
    And, by all likelihood, some cheer is toward.   *Knocks.*
GRE: They're busy within; you were best knock louder.
             Pedant looks out of the window.
PED: What's he that knocks as he would beat down the gate?
15 VIN: Is Signior Lucentio within, sir?
PED: He's within, sir, but not to be spoken withal.
VIN: What if a man bring him a hundred pound or two, to
    make merry withal?
PED: Keep your hundred pounds to yourself: he shall need
20 none, so long as I live.
PET: Nay, I told you your son was well beloved in Padua. Do

[1]*over*

79

you hear, sir? To leave frivolous circumstances, I pray
you, tell Signior Lucentio that his father is come from
Pisa, and is here at the door to speak with him.

PED:　Thou liest: his father is come from Padua and here

25　　looking out at the window.

VIN:　Art thou his father?

PED:　Ay, sir; so his mother says, if I may believe her.

PET:　Why, how now, gentleman! why, this is flat knavery,
to take upon you another man's name.

30　PED:　Lay hands on the villain: I believe a' means to cozen
somebody in this city under my countenance.

Enter Biondello.

BIO:　I have seen them in the church together:
God send 'em good shipping! But who is here? mine
old master Vincentio! now we are undone and brought

35　　to nothing.

VIN: Come hither, crack-hemp.[2]

BIO: I hope I may choose, sir.

VIN:　Come hither, you rogue. What, have you forgot me?

BIO: Forgot you! no, sir: I could not forget you, for I never

40　　saw you before in all my life.

VIN:　What, you notorious villain, didst thou never see thy
master's father, Vincentio?

BIO: What, my old worshipful old master? yes, marry, sir:
see where he looks out of the window.

45　VIN:　Is't so, indeed?　　　　　　　　*He beats Biondello.*

BIO: Help, help, help! here's a madman will murder me.
　　　　　　　　　　　　　　　　　　　[Exit.]

PED:　Help, son! help, Signior Baptista!　*[Exit from above.]*

PET: Prithee, Kate, let's stand aside and see the end of this
controversy.

Enter Pedant [below] with servants, Baptista, Tranio.

50　TRA:　Sir, what are you that offer to beat my servant?

VIN:　What am I, sir! nay, what are you, sir? O immortal
gods! O fine villain! A silken doublet! a velvet hose!
a scarlet cloak! and a copatain[3] hat! O, I am undone!
I am undone! while I play the good husband at home,

55　　my son and my servant spend all at the university.

TRA: How now! what's the matter?

BAP: What, is the man lunatic?

TRA: Sir, you seem a sober ancient gentleman by your habit,
but your words show you a madman. Why, sir, what
60   'cerns it you if I wear pearl and gold? I thank my good
father, I am able to maintain it.

VIN: Thy father! O villain! he is a sailmaker in Bergamo.[4]

BAP: You mistake, sir, you mistake, sir. Pray, what do you
think is his name?

65 VIN: His name! as if I knew not his name: I have brought
him up ever since he was three years old, and his name is
Tranio.

PED: Away, away, mad ass! his name is Lucentio and he
is mine only son, and heir to the lands of me, Signior
70   Vincentio.

VIN: Lucentio! O, he hath murdered his master!
Lay hold on him, I charge you, in the duke's name. O,
my son, my son! Tell me, thou villain, where is my son
Lucentio?

75 TRA: Call forth an officer.

Enter an Officer.

Carry this mad knave to the gaol.[5] Father Baptista, I
charge you see that he be forthcoming.

VIN: Carry me to the gaol!

GRE: Stay, officer: he shall not go to prison.

80 BAP: Talk not, Signior Gremio: I say he shall go to prison.

GRE: Take heed, Signior Baptista, lest you be cony-catched in
this business: I dare swear this is the right Vincentio.

PED: Swear, if thou darest.

GRE: Nay, I dare not swear it.

85 TRA: Then thou wert best say that I am not Lucentio.

GRE: Yes, I know thee to be Signior Lucentio.

BAP: Away with the dotard![6] to the gaol with him!

Enter Biondello, Lucentio and Bianca.

VIN: Thus strangers may be hailed and abused:
O monstrous villain!

90 BIO: O! we are spoiled and—yonder he is: deny him, forswear
him, or else we are all undone.

[4] *a city northeast of Milan*

[5] *jail*

[6] *fool*

Exeunt Biondello, Tranio and Pedant as fast as may be.

LUC: Pardon, sweet father.   *Kneel.*

VIN: Lives my sweet son?

BIA: Pardon, dear father.

95 BAP: How hast thou offended?
       Where is Lucentio?

LUC: Here's Lucentio,
       Right son to the right Vincentio;
       That have by marriage made thy daughter mine,

100   While counterfeit supposes[7] bleared thine eyne.[8]

GRE: Here's packing,[9] with a witness to deceive us all!

VIN: Where is that damned villain Tranio,
       That faced and braved me in this matter so?

BAP: Why, tell me, is not this my Cambio?

105 BIA: Cambio is changed into Lucentio.

LUC: Love wrought these miracles. Bianca's love
       Made me exchange my state with Tranio,
       While he did bear my countenance in the town;
       And happily I have arrived at the last

110   Unto the wished haven of my bliss.
       What Tranio did, myself enforced him to;
       Then pardon him, sweet father, for my sake.

VIN: I'll slit the villain's nose, that would have sent me to
       the gaol.

115 BAP: But do you hear, sir? have you married my daughter
       without asking my good will?

VIN: Fear not, Baptista; we will content you, go to: but I
       will in, to be revenged for this villainy.   *Exit.*

BAP: And I, to sound the depth of this knavery.   *Exit.*

120 LUC: Look not pale, Bianca; thy father will not frown.
                              Exeunt [Lucentio and Bianca.]

GRE: My cake is dough; but I'll in among the rest,
       Out of hope of all, but my share of the feast. *[Exit]*

KAT: Husband, let's follow, to see the end of this ado.

PET: First kiss me, Kate, and we will.

125 KAT: What, in the midst of the street?

PET: What, art thou ashamed of me?

KAT: No, sir, God forbid; but ashamed to kiss.

PET: Why, then let's home again. Come, sirrah, let's away.

[7]*beliefs*

[8]*eyes*

[9]*plotting*

KAT: Nay, I will give thee a kiss: now pray thee, love, stay.
130 PET: Is not this well? Come, my sweet Kate:
    Better once than never, for never too late.

Exeunt.

SCENE II
[Padua. Lucentio's house.]

*Enter Baptista, Vincentio, Gremio, the Pedant, Lucentio, and
Bianca. [Petruchio, Katharina, Hortensio,] Tranio, Biondello,
Grumio, and Widow. The Serving men with Tranio bringing in
a Banquet.*

LUC: At last, though long, our jarring notes agree:
    And time it is, when raging war is done,
    To smile at scapes and perils overblown.
    My fair Bianca, bid my father welcome,
5   While I with self-same kindness welcome thine.
    Brother Petruchio, sister Katharina,
    And thou, Hortensio, with thy loving widow,
    Feast with the best, and welcome to my house:
    My banquet is to close our stomachs up,
10   After our great good cheer. Pray you, sit down;
    For now we sit to chat as well as eat.
PET: Nothing but sit and sit, and eat and eat!
BAP: Padua affords this kindness, son Petruchio.
PET: Padua affords nothing but what is kind.
15 HOR: For both our sakes, I would that word were true.
PET: Now, for my life, Hortensio fears his widow.
WID: Then never trust me, if I be afeard.
PET: You are very sensible, and yet you miss my sense:
    I mean, Hortensio is afeard of you.
20 WID: He that is giddy thinks the world turns round.
PET: Roundly replied.
KAT: Mistress, how mean you that?
WID: Thus I conceive[10] by him.
PET: Conceives[11] by me! How likes Hortensio that?
25 HOR: My widow says, thus she conceives her tale.

[10]*conclude from*

[11]*becomes pregnant*

PET: Very well mended. Kiss him for that, good widow.

KAT: 'He that is giddy thinks the world turns round:'
    I pray you, tell me what you meant by that.

WID: Your husband, being troubled with a shrew,

30   Measures my husband's sorrow by his woe:
    And now you know my meaning.

KAT: A very mean meaning.

WID: Right, I mean you.

KAT: And I am mean indeed, respecting you.

35 PET: To her, Kate!

HOR: To her, widow!

PET: A hundred marks, my Kate does put her down.

HOR: That's my office.

PET: Spoke like an officer; ha' to thee, lad!

                    Drinks to Hortensio.

40 BAP: How likes Gremio these quick-witted folks?

GRE: Believe me, sir, they butt together well.

BIA: Head, and butt! an hasty-witted body
    Would say your head and butt were head and horn.[12]

VIN: Ay, mistress bride, hath that awaken'd you?

45 BIA: Ay, but not frighted me; therefore I'll sleep again.

PET: Nay, that you shall not: since you have begun,
    Have at you for a bitter jest or two!

BIA: Am I your bird? I mean to shift my bush;
    And then pursue me as you draw your bow.

50   You are welcome all.

            Exit Bianca [Katharina, and Widow.]

PET: She hath prevented me. Here, Signior Tranio.
    This bird you aim'd at, though you hit her not;
    Therefore a health to all that shot and miss'd.

TRA: O, sir, Lucentio slipp'd me like his greyhound,

55   Which runs himself and catches for his master.

PET: A good swift simile, but something currish.

TRA: 'Tis well, sir, that you hunted for yourself:
    'Tis thought your deer does hold you at a bay.

BAP: O ho, Petruchio! Tranio hits you now.

60 LUC: I thank thee for that gird, good Tranio.

HOR: Confess, confess, hath he not hit you here?

PET: A' has a little gall'd me, I confess;
    And, as the jest did glance away from me,
    'Tis ten to one it maim'd you two outright.

[12]*the horn of a cuckold*

65 BAP: Now, in good sadness, son Petruchio,
          I think thou hast the veriest shrew of all.
     PET: Well, I say no: and therefore for assurance
          Let's each one send unto his wife;
          And he whose wife is most obedient
70   To come at first when he doth send for her,
          Shall win the wager which we will propose.
     HOR: Content. What is the wager?
     LUC: Twenty crowns.
     PET: Twenty crowns!
75   I'll venture so much of my hawk or hound,
          But twenty times so much upon my wife.
     LUC: A hundred then.
     HOR: Content.
     PET: A match! 'tis done.
80 HOR: Who shall begin?
     LUC: That will I.
          Go, Biondello, bid your mistress come to me.
     BIO: I go.   *Exit.*
     BAP: Son, I'll be your half, Bianca comes.
85 LUC: I'll have no halves; I'll bear it all myself.

Enter Biondello.
          How now! what news?
     BIO: Sir, my mistress sends you word
          That she is busy and she cannot come.
     PET: How! she is busy and she cannot come!
90   Is that an answer?
     GRE: Ay, and a kind one too:
          Pray God, sir, your wife send you not a worse.
     PET: I hope better.
     HOR: Sirrah Biondello, go and entreat my wife
95   To come to me forthwith.   *Exit Biondello.*
     PET: O, ho! entreat her!
          Nay, then she must needs come.
     HOR: I am afraid, sir, do what you can.

Enter Biondello.
          Yours will not be entreated: Now, where's my wife?
100 BIO: She says you have some goodly jest in hand:
          She will not come: she bids you come to her.

PET: Worse and worse; she will not come! O vile,
    Intolerable, not to be endured!
    Sirrah Grumio, go to your mistress;
105   Say, I command her to come to me.   *Exit [Grumio.]*
HOR: I know her answer.
PET: What?
HOR: She will not.
PET: The fouler fortune mine, and there an end.
110 BAP: Now, by my holidame,[13] here comes Katharina!

13*"holy dame," i.e., the Virgin Mary*

Enter Katharina.
KAT: What is your will, sir, that you send for me?
PET: Where is your sister, and Hortensio's wife?
KAT: They sit conferring by the parlor fire.
PET: Go fetch them hither: if they deny to come,
115   Swinge[14] me them soundly forth unto their husbands:
    Away, I say, and bring them hither straight.
                    [Exit Katharina.]

14*whip*

LUC: Here is a wonder, if you talk of a wonder.
HOR: And so it is: I wonder what it bodes.
PET: Marry, peace it bodes, and love and quiet life,
120   And awful rule and right supremacy;
    And, to be short, what not, that's sweet and happy?
BAP: Now, fair befal thee, good Petruchio!
    The wager thou hast won; and I will add
    Unto their losses twenty thousand crowns;
125   Another dowry to another daughter,
    For she is changed, as she had never been.
PET: Nay, I will win my wager better yet
    And show more sign of her obedience,
    Her new-built virtue and obedience.
130   See where she comes and brings your froward wives
    As prisoners to her womanly persuasion.

Enter Kate, Bianca, and Widow.
    Katharina, that cap of yours becomes you not:
    Off with that bauble, throw it under-foot.
WID: Lord, let me never have a cause to sigh,
135   Till I be brought to such a silly pass!
BIA: Fie! what a foolish duty call you this?

Luc: I would your duty were as foolish too:
     The wisdom of your duty, fair Bianca,
     Hath cost me an hundred crowns since supper-time.

140 Bia: The more fool you, for laying[15] on my duty.

    Pet: Katharina, I charge thee, tell these headstrong women
     What duty they do owe their lords and husbands.

  Wid: Come, come, you're mocking: we will have no telling.

    Pet: Come on, I say; and first begin with her.

145 Wid: She shall not.

    Pet: I say she shall: and first begin with her.

    Kat: Fie, fie! unknit that threatening unkind brow,
     And dart not scornful glances from those eyes,
     To wound thy lord, thy king, thy governor:

150   It blots thy beauty as frosts do bite the meads,
     Confounds thy fame as whirlwinds shake fair buds,
     And in no sense is meet[16] or amiable.
     A woman moved is like a fountain troubled,
     Muddy, ill-seeming, thick, bereft of beauty;

155   And while it is so, none so dry or thirsty
     Will deign to sip or touch one drop of it.
     Thy husband is thy lord, thy life, thy keeper,
     Thy head, thy sovereign; one that cares for thee,
     And for thy maintenance commits his body

160   To painful labour both by sea and land,
     To watch the night in storms, the day in cold,
     Whilst thou liest warm at home, secure and safe;
     And craves no other tribute at thy hands
     But love, fair looks and true obedience;

165   Too little payment for so great a debt.
     Such duty as the subject owes the prince
     Even such a woman oweth to her husband;
     And when she is froward, peevish, sullen, sour,
     And not obedient to his honest will,

170   What is she but a foul contending rebel
     And graceless traitor to her loving lord?
     I am ashamed that women are so simple
     To offer war where they should kneel for peace;
     Or seek for rule, supremacy and sway,

175   When they are bound to serve, love and obey.
     Why are our bodies soft and weak and smooth,

[15]*betting*

[16]*fitting*

       Unapt to toil and trouble in the world,

       But that our soft conditions and our hearts

       Should well agree with our external parts?

180   Come, come, you froward and unable worms!

       My mind hath been as big as one of yours,

       My heart as great, my reason haply more,

       To bandy word for word and frown for frown;

       But now I see our lances are but straws,

185   Our strength as weak, our weakness past compare,

       That seeming to be most which we indeed least are.

       Then vail[17] your stomachs,[18] for it is no boot,

       And place your hands below your husband's foot:

       In token of which duty, if he please,

190   My hand is ready; may it do him ease.

PET: Why, there's a wench! Come on, and kiss me, Kate.

LUC: Well, go thy ways, old lad; for thou shalt ha't.

VIN: 'Tis a good hearing when children are toward.

LUC: But a harsh hearing when women are froward.

195 PET: Come, Kate, we'll to bed.

       We three are married, but you two are sped.

       To Lucentio.

       'Twas I won the wager, though you hit the white;

       And, being a winner, God give you good night!

                  Exeunt Petruchio and Katharina.

HOR: Now, go thy ways; thou hast tamed a curst shrew.

200 LUC: 'Tis a wonder, by your leave, she will be tamed so.

                          Exeunt.

[17] *suppress*

[18] *willfulness*

Vocabulary and Glossary

Induction, Scene I

pair of stocks – The *stocks* were wooden posts with holes into which a prisoner's head and feet would be locked.

Richard Conqueror – Sly attempts to trace his family to William the Conqueror (c.1027-1087), the king who first united England.

Go by, Jeronimy – an expression meaning "Go on with you"

sirrah – a term for a person of lower rank

anon – soon

spleen – enthusiasm

Induction, Scene II

Semiramis – a queen legendary for her love of luxury and her erotic appeal; the Lord promises Sly a couch luxurious enough for such a queen.

"Dost thou love pictures?" – All the pictures the servants offer Sly are of romantic scenes from Greek mythology.

Adonis – Aphrodite, who was in love with Adonis, hid in the *sedges* (tall plants growing by the water) and watched him.

Io – Because Zeus was in love with Io, he turned her into a cow to hide her from his jealous wife, Hera.

Daphne – a young woman pursued by Apollo (god of wisdom and light) through a forest; as she ran, she prayed for protection to her father, a river god, who turned her into a laurel tree.

Act I, Scene I

Stoics – followers of a Greek philosophy that stresses emotional control and upright morals; Tranio is urging Lucentio to not be so studious that he neglects to have fun. He plays on the similarity in sound between "stoics" and "stocks" (dull people).

Ovid – a Roman love poet (43 B.C.-c.18 A.D.); his poem *Ars Amatoria* (*The Art of Love*) will be mentioned later in the play.

cart – to parade her around in a cart (the usual punishment for prostitution)

Minerva – the Roman goddess of learning and the arts

Anna – sister of and confidante to Dido, queen of Carthage, in the Roman poet Vergil's epic *Aeneid*; in a famous passage, Dido confesses to Anna that she is in love with the Trojan warrior Aeneas.

queen of Carthage – Dido

"Redime te...minimo" – lines from a Latin grammar book commonly used in Shakespeare's time

daughter of Agenor – Europa, a lovely young woman whom Jove, disguised as a beautiful cow, seduced; when he knelt down, she climbed on his back, and he swam away with her.

Cretan – of or relating to the island of Crete (southeast of Greece), from which Europa was abducted

Act I, Scene II

two and thirty, a pip out – a play on the name of a popular card game called "one and thirty"; Grumio is saying that Petruchio is one "pip," or point, over his limit, in other words, drunk.

Florentius – a knight described in the poet John Gower's (c.1325-1408) *Confessio Amantis*; the knight promises to marry an ugly old woman in exchange for the answer to a riddle. She then turns into a beautiful young woman.

Sibyl – in classical mythology, a priestess to whom Apollo granted eternal life, but not eternal youth; she is often represented as an ancient woman

Adriatic – an arm of the Mediterranean Ocean between the Balkan peninsula and Italy

jade – literally, a worn-out horse; slang for "worthless fellow"

Hercules – In classical mythology, Hercules is considered the strongest man in the world; as punishment for an accidental murder, he was forced to do twelve difficult labors (also referred to as Alcides).

Act II, Scene I

"I'll fume with them…" – Kate has punned on the word "frets" (meaning both "the note indications on a musical instrument" and "gets upset") and "fume" ("to get upset, to rage").

banns – in some Christian churches, announcements of an intended marriage that are made over several consecutive Sundays

herald – an extended pun based on *heraldry* (a system of symbols used by wealthy families); when Kate says that Petruchio will lose his *arms* (coat of arms, the symbol of a gentleman) if he strikes her, he begs her to put him in her herald's books (books that explain coats of arms and the genealogy of well-born families).

Dian – Diana, goddess of chastity and the hunt

Grissel – Griselda, a woman whose faithfulness was tested by her husband; the story is told by both the English poet Chaucer and the Italian poet Boccaccio.

Lucrece – Lucretia was a Roman woman who, according to the poet Livy, killed herself to preserve her honor after being raped; the story was told by Shakespeare in a well-known poem "The Rape of Lucrece."

vied – out-wagered; Petruchio says that Kate, like a gambler desperate to win, kept promising him more and more things.

"venture madly on a desperate mart" – i.e., made a risky bet on something (Kate) that is not easy to get rid of

quiet in the match – a peaceful marriage

Tyrian – Tyre, in North Africa, was famous for its purple dye.

road – harbor

Act III, Scene I

patroness – Minerva, the Roman goddess of wisdom, crafts, and music

breeching scholar – Bianca is saying that she is not a young or beginner student; she is also using *breech* as meaning that she is not young enough 'to be whipped.'

"Hic ibat...celsa senis." – a quote from Ovid's *Heroides*

pantaloon – Pantaloons were loose-fitting trousers often worn by old men; they therefore became a symbol of senility or foolishness.

fie – an oath expressing contempt

Æacides – Ajax, a Greek warrior who appears in the *Heroides*

rudiments – basic principles

gamut – musical scales in which notes are represented by sounds (do, re, mi, etc.); Hortensio gives Bianca a paper on which he has supposedly written a poem to help her remember the gamut. He has actually hidden a love letter between the lines.

Act III, Scene II

possessed with the glanders – Biondello, in this passage full of comical overstatement, lists numerous diseases that the broken-down horse seems to have.

glanders – a contagious disease in which spreading pimples or blisters form under the skin

to mose in the chine – to have a hurt spine because of glanders

lampass – a disease affecting a horse's mouth

fashions – a form of glanders that occurs on the surface of the skin

wind-galls – soft tumors that form on the leg

spavins – a swelling of the leg joints

yellows – jaundice (discoloration of the skin due to liver malfunction)

fives – a disease that affects the glands in the throat; also called *strangles*

staggers – a disease involving dizziness and unsteadiness

bots – worms

restrained – pulled tight

lackey – a slave, servant

gartered – belted

"humor of forty fancies" – i.e., the result of a thousand different impulses

footboy – a footservant

mean-apparell'd – shabbily dressed

gallants – gentlemen
wherefore – why
doff – to remove
habit – an outfit
digress – to deviate, depart (i.e., break my promise)
excuse – to explain
unreverent – disrespectful
skills – matters
vantage – an advantage
list – want

The Folio edition of *The Taming of the Shrew* ends Act II here, but most modern
   editions don't.

Act IV, Scene I

horn – A cuckold (a man cheated on by his wife) was usually pictured with
   horns. Bianca uses the same insult against Gremio in Act V, Scene II.
Jack, boy! – a *catch*, or refrain, from a popular song; Curtis puns on the word
   catch in the next line.
miry – swampy
pluck my foot – take off my boot
awry – incorrectly
choler – According to a theory popular from ancient to Elizabethan times, bodi-
   ly fluids called *humors* determine a person's mood and character. An excess
   of yellow bile makes a person *choleric* (angry and vengeful); too much black
   bile results in a *melancholy*, or depressed, personality; an abundance of
   phlegm (mucus) makes for a sluggish and dull nature, called *phlegmatic*; and
   too much blood results in a *sanguine*, or cheerful, type.
"My falcon is now sharp and passing empty…" – Petruchio uses an extended
   metaphor to compare Kate to a falcon (or *haggard*). Until she *stoops* (flies
   directly to her keeper, Petruchio), she will not be *full-gorged* (allowed to eat
   her fill); he believes that unless she is hungry, she will pay no attention to
   her *lure* (bait used to recall a hawk). He will *watch* her (i.e., keep her awake)
   just as a keeper does not allow high-strung or disobedient birds to sleep, in
   the hope of wearing them out.

Act IV, Scene II

Art to Love – Ovid's *Ars Amatoria* was a "handbook" for men and women seek-
   ing love.
Tripoli – the capitol of Libya, in North Africa

Act IV, Scene III

"hop me over every kennel home" – i.e., "take a flying leap"

"thou thread, thou thimble" – Petruchio insults the tailor by describing him with a tailor's units of measurement. A *quarter* is a fourth of a yard; a *nail* is a sixteenth of a yard. A *quantity*, like a *remnant*, is a leftover scrap of cloth. Petruchio also promises to *bemete* (both "measure," as a tailor measures cloth, and "measure out punishment upon") the tailor.

Act IV, Scene IV

"cum privilegio ad imprimendum solum" – [*Latin*] "with the sole right to print"; Biondello is saying that Lucentio should "take assurance" (i.e., have intercourse) with Bianca as soon as possible, so that no other man puts his "stamp" on her.

Act V, Scene I

—

Act V, Scene II

—

Insightful and Reader-Friendly, Yet Affordable

Prestwick House Literary Touchstone Classic Editions–
The Editions By Which All Others May Be Judged

Every *Prestwick House Literary Touchstone Classic* is enhanced with Reading Pointers for Sharper Insight to improve comprehension and provide insights that will help students recognize key themes, symbols, and plot complexities. In addition, each title includes a Glossary of the more difficult words and concepts.

For the Shakespeare titles, along with the Reading Pointers and Glossary, we include margin notes and various strategies to understanding the language of Shakespeare.

New titles are constantly being added; call or visit our website for current listing.

Special Educator's Discount – At Least

50% Off

		Retail Price	Educator's Discount
200053	Adventures of Huckleberry Finn	~~$4.99~~	**$2.49**
202118	Antigone	~~$3.99~~	**$1.99**
200141	Awakening, The	~~$5.99~~	**$2.99**
200179	Christmas Carol, A	~~$3.99~~	**$1.99**
200694	Doll's House, A	~~$3.99~~	**$1.99**
200054	Frankenstein	~~$4.99~~	**$1.99**
200091	Hamlet	~~$3.99~~	**$1.99**
200074	Heart of Darkness	~~$3.99~~	**$1.99**
200147	Importance of Being Earnest, The	~~$3.99~~	**$1.99**
200146	Julius Caesar	~~$3.99~~	**$1.99**
200125	Macbeth	~~$3.99~~	**$1.99**
200081	Midsummer Night's Dream, A	~~$3.99~~	**$1.99**
200079	Narrative of the Life of Frederick Douglass	~~$3.99~~	**$1.99**
200564	Oedipus Rex	~~$3.99~~	**$1.99**
200095	Othello	~~$3.99~~	**$1.99**
200193	Romeo and Juliet	~~$3.99~~	**$0.99**
200132	Scarlet Letter, The	~~$5.99~~	**$2.99**
200251	Tale of Two Cities, A	~~$6.99~~	**$3.49**

Prestwick House

Prestwick House, Inc. • P.O. Box 658, Clayton, DE 19938
Phone (800) 932-4593 • Fax (888) 718-9333 • www.prestwickhouse.com

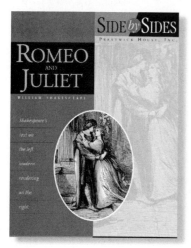